Community Action Rooted in History

THE Civi**Connections** MODEL OF SERVICE-LEARNING

NCSS
Bulletin 106

Edited by
Rahima C. Wade

National Council for the Social Studies

8555 Sixteenth Street • Suite 500 • Silver Spring, Maryland 20910

www.**socialstudies**.org

Editorial staff on this publication: Michael Simpson, Chi Yang
Design/Production: Cowan Creative, www.cowancreative.com

Library of Congress Control Number: 2007929591
ISBN: 978-0-87986-100-1

Printed in the United States of America

5 4 3 2 1

Table of Contents

This publication was supported by the Public Health Service and National Council for the Social Studies under Corporation for National and Community Service Grant No. 03KCHMD002 (Prime Award Number). Its contents are solely the responsibility of the authors and do not necessarily represent the official views of the CNCS or National Council for the Social Studies.

Introduction

RAHIMA C. WADE

The mission of social studies education is informed and active citizenship, yet how often do our students get the opportunity to apply skills and knowledge learned in our social studies classes to taking action in their communities? With the proliferation of service-learning programs nationally, more students are venturing out of the classroom to work on environmental problems or help those in need. Yet seldom are these efforts connected to the subject matter of the social studies curriculum. Typically, students learn history, geography, and economics content in their social studies classes separate from their participation in service-learning as a graduation requirement, extracurricular activity, or extra-credit assignment in other courses.

The CiviConnections program was developed to give students the opportunity to learn local and national history as a means for informing civic action via service and advocacy in the local community. Rather than separating historical content and service-learning, CiviConnections brought together these two unlikely partners and found in their alliance a surprising and mutually rewarding compatibility. With the promise of making a difference about real issues that students care about, investigating the local historical roots of a social or environmental problem took on new meaning. And service based on understanding the history of efforts to make a difference led to students taking informed action with the potential for significant impact.

In the past three years, more than 250 elementary through high school teachers from New York to Hawaii participated in the CiviConnections program. With federal funding from the Corporation for National and Community Service granted to National Council for the Social Studies, teacher teams from school districts in more than 25 states and U.S. territories have developed meaningful opportunities for more than 8,000 students to choose an issue they care about, investigate the history of the issue, and become "history makers" themselves as they worked on educating others and serving their communities. Even though the period in which the project was funded has now drawn to a close, these teacher teams will continue to apply the principles of the project to their service-learning endeavors. More information on CiviConnections activities and workshop training are available from the Editor of this Bulletin, Rahima Wade (rahima-wade@uiowa.edu).

This Bulletin chronicles some of the exciting projects these teachers and students have created. If you are a social studies teacher reading this Bulletin, we hope you will be inspired by these stories of engaging and meaningful social studies teaching, and that you will want to develop your own similar project.

Part 1 provides an overview of the two key elements in the CiviConnections program. *Toward a Usable Past*, by Linda Levstik, illuminates the process of local historical inquiry with relevant questions and pointers for classroom practice. The second chapter in this section, *Community Service-Learning for Democratic Citizenship*, provides a rationale for the presence of service-learning in social studies education and an overview of the essential elements of high-quality community service-learning.

Part 2 details the six steps that comprise a CiviConnections project and provides a blueprint for creating a project that will meet your students' interests, your curricular requirements, and your community's needs. The chapters in this part of the Bulletin provide practical strategies for developing a project that is uniquely suited to your teaching situation.

In Part 3, the stories of ten CiviConnections projects illustrate how students made significant contributions to their communities with support from their teachers, parents, local community agencies, and the media. In the first chapter in this section, several stories on projects related to poverty and hunger demonstrate how projects focused on the same issue unfold in similar and different ways. Other chapters in this section highlight projects on a variety of issues unique to each of the communities in which they were created.

The conclusion highlights the central themes in successful CiviConnections projects, essentially providing a detailed checklist for creating a project that engages students' enthusiasm and potential, meets critical community needs, and satisfies local and state curricular requirements.

There are many people whose contributions were essential to bringing about this Bulletin on the CiviConnections program. Funding was provided by both the federal Corporation for National and Community Service, as well as National

Council for the Social Studies. I would especially like to thank my collaborator, Dr. Linda Levstik, for her contributions, not only to this Bulletin, but also to the ongoing development of the program and to the summer workshops during the first two years. In the third year, Dr. Lynne Boyle-Baise willingly served as a co-presenter, for which I am very grateful. In addition, Michael Simpson and the staff in the NCSS publications department were very supportive of this effort to bring the CiviConnections program to social studies teachers nationally. I also cannot overlook the efforts of the National Council for the Social Studies staff who have contributed many hours to the program, notably Treverne Brown-Thomas, Carlos Herndon, Prema Parmar, Paul Schwobel, and Ana Post. I also wish to express my gratitude to the Corporation for National and Community Service's Learn and Serve America Program for the federal funding that supported CiviConnections between 2003 and 2007.

Finally, this Bulletin would not have been possible without the many hours of innovation and effort contributed by more than 270 teachers and their students who implemented CiviConnections in their classrooms and communities. These teachers were willing to jump into a new program and give it their all, in spite of challenges with time, curriculum standards, and financial issues. This book is dedicated to them, in honor of their creative spirit and their willingness to do what it takes to make a difference for their students and their communities.

Part One
Laying the Foundations

CHAPTER ONE

In Pursuit of a Usable Past

Linda S. Levstik

I could have entitled this chapter *A Guide for the Perplexed*, after the writings of the medieval rabbi and philosopher Maimonides, because our students are often perplexed by history, at least as it appears in classroom lectures and dry-as-toast textbooks.[1] We developed CiviConnections as one response to that perplexity, encouraging teachers and students to identify historical roots of local problems in order to work more intelligently for the common good.

From our perspective, history—or, better yet, histories—frame citizens' understanding of shared institutions and shared problems. Because some groups and individuals struggle to register in the public imagination or to be accounted for in civic and civil discourse, the depth and accuracy of constructions of our own and others' histories have important consequences for civic decision-making.

Thus, fulfilling the mission of social studies to create informed and active citizens depends in part on how we help students make sense of historical information. How can we help students understand the roots of current issues? Under what circumstances will students consider a problem from different historical and contemporary perspectives? In sum, how can students develop a usable past—a past that helps them negotiate issues and exercise agency in the give and take of a pluralist democracy? While historical study serves a number of purposes in public schools, informing civic engagement remains one of its most significant goals. Too often, however, students miss the connections between history in schools and historically informed civic agency. The CiviConnections program has offered one approach to making such links more explicit.

Current Issues, Historical Roots

Identifying historic roots of current issues cannot, alone, encourage tolerance and understanding of differences, guarantee that citizens will engage in democratic discourse, or empower student-citizens to exercise agency either in their own communities or, eventually, at the ballot box and beyond. Rather, historical investigations offer student-citizens the opportunity

to alleviate current problems based on informed collective deliberation.[2] With appropriate scaffolding, historical inquiry encourages students to withhold judgment (and action) pending consideration of evidence from multiple perspectives and multiple sources. Following careful inquiry, a deliberation phase challenges students to consider the pros and cons of alternative courses of action. As Parker notes, "the array of alternatives that a diverse group generates, assuming participants are both speaking and listening, will be broader than one could accomplish working alone. The resulting decision will be better than if many alternatives were overlooked."[3]

Not all issues offer appropriate avenues for student inquiry or agency. Sometimes an inquiry requires a degree of expertise students lack; in other cases, the resources are simply insufficient to support inquiry. For instance, older students investigating urban development might reasonably be expected to investigate the historical roots of eminent domain, while for younger students, documenting the changing face or historical significance of a particular building might be more appropriate. Together, however, both groups might collaborate on preserving a neighborhood youth center from demolition by arguing for its place on the historic register. On the other hand, preservation of the youth center might be worthwhile and supportable on some grounds, but available historical data may not provide an argument for the historic registry. In still other instances, the historical resources may be rich and interesting, but the opportunity for informed agency, at least in the form of direct service, might be limited.

As you read through this book, you will learn how middle and high school teachers and students identify appropriate historical resources to support disciplined inquiry in order to exercise informed agency. Disciplined inquiry refers to purposeful investigations that employ the goals, standards, and procedures of historical study: question-setting, finding information, evaluating sources, reconciling conflicting accounts, and creating an interpretive account.[4] Informed agency brings the results of disciplined inquiry to bear on communal deliberations aimed at alleviating communal problems. Ultimately, our goal in this book is to encourage informed agency. This chapter focuses on the disciplined inquiry that makes informed agency possible.

Connecting Disciplined Inquiry to Informed Agency
The Importance of Questions

The human desire for simple answers to complex problems often results in misunderstandings, missed opportunities, inappropriate "solutions," and misdirected agency. Students often engage in school-initiated service projects (e.g., collecting food, cleaning up the school yard, or planting a garden), yet less often do we, as teachers, ask the kinds of questions that might help students develop a better or deeper sense of their experience or develop more useful projects. Without solid questions in mind, it becomes difficult to decide whether a particular service project actually serves anyone, much less whether it can or should be maintained over time. Conducting disciplined inquiry into the connections between past and present circumstances, however, makes it more likely that students' agency—in this case, their choices about direct and indirect service and advocacy efforts—will actually help to alleviate a problem. We cannot assume, however, that students will make those connections on their own. Instead, disciplined inquiry must be taught, beginning with careful attention to the kinds of questions that guide inquiry and inform agency.

Current events can certainly generate interesting and challenging historical questions that might motivate inquiry into and deliberation about changing conceptions of the common good. In one school, current controversies over immigration and flood relief spurred questions such as, "How have Americans responded to immigration in the past?" "Why are southern border-crossings more controversial than crossings along our northern border?" "How have communities dealt with natural disasters in the past?" and "What responses have been effective in our community?" In another school, students complained about the lack of recreation opportunities in their small mining community, and generated questions about how recreational opportunities changed after the "model coal camp" was no longer a company-run town. Similarly, news reports of crowded conditions in a local shelter led a group of eighth graders to ask questions about the roots of homelessness and how their community responded to these problems in the past. As you read through the projects described in this book, you will find an array of guiding questions. Good historical questions can make the difference between a successful and unsuccessful service-learning experience. As you look over the questions in this book, think about:

- What kinds of activity generated the question(s) for historical inquiry? Sometimes teachers introduce a topic for discussion. In other cases, they arrange an initiating activity such as a simulation, documentary, guest speaker, or digital movie that provokes interest and generates questions.
- What kinds of questions frame the historical inquiry? Sometimes an inquiry begins with a single question. A group of students at one school, for example, began by asking how their community had gone from the Chinese Exclusion Act to being a tourist destination. In other cases, students generate a number of questions related to an issue. Fifth graders studying the early Republic wondered why so few people today vote in elections. They set out to investigate several past/present comparisons: How have rules about voting changed over time? How has who votes changed over time? Are people more likely to vote in local or national elections now? In the past? How have people been encouraged to vote in the past and now?
- Do questions pass the "so what" test? So what if students learn the answers to these questions? Are they worth student (and teacher) time and effort? Do they relate at all to curricular requirements, capitalize on cross-disciplinary possibilities, deepen students' understanding of important content, skills, attitudes, and values, or point towards student-appropriate civic engagement?
- What kinds of inquiry can these questions support? Which require factual answers? Which call for opinions, and whose opinions? What words or terms might require definition before a question can be investigated intelligently?
- Do questions adequately address an issue or topic? Sometimes students generate "domino" questions. One question sets off a flurry of imitators and the questions devolve into what one group of third graders labeled "ridiculous" questions—impossible to answer and not worth the trouble to try. In other cases, questions miss important perspectives. The questions about voting, for instance, might miss the fact that voting rights have expanded and contracted over time. At one point, for instance, women in New Jersey had the right to vote, but that was rescinded until passage of national women's suffrage. Similarly, questions about homelessness might not uncover issues about deinstitutionalization, unless students specifically ask how people become homeless.

In the other chapters in this book, you will notice different kinds of questions and different approaches to generating them. In each case, though, projects work best when service-learning tightly links historical questions to evidence: primary and secondary sources that students analyze for reliability, perspective, and relevance to the questions at hand.

Crucial Work with Evidence

Most students have little experience with identifying and analyzing resources, and find it especially challenging to develop evidence-based historical interpretations, much less use those interpretations to argue for civic action. It helps to consider your students as apprentices who need structure to help organize their work and models of good practice. As teachers, we need to ask students probing questions, help them try out different practices and procedures, and provide critical feedback on their work.[5]

If left to their own devices to investigate historical questions, students will head first for the Internet. Because flailing about in cyberspace wastes an incredible amount of time, we will find it worthwhile to provide our students with initial "archives." These source packets include several types of data, appropriate websites, and some graphic organizers to help students sift through the data. A packet on child labor, for instance, might include a sample of Lewis Hines' photographs (and the web address for the online collection of his work); recent photographs of child laborers in different industries and different countries; political cartoons; statements from advocates for child labor, reformers, government inspectors, and "whistle blowers"; along with some guiding questions to help students sort through the sources. In planning the archives, think about differentiating instruction to provide different kinds of sources at different levels of difficulty so that all students can be involved at some level. At this point, keep sources relatively brief. Sources should motivate additional research, not intimidate or paralyze students by their sheer volume.

As students begin their work with the archives, it helps for small groups to sort sources into categories by time period, type of labor, perspective, and so forth. A large classroom timeline can be particularly useful here, especially if you can move things easily on the timeline. (Velcro® strips work well.) It also helps if each group selects one source to share with the whole class, discussing the type of source, the kinds of questions it might help answer, new questions it might raise, and other sources or ideas that it might contradict or support. In some classes, we can select a single source for discussion. This might be a new type of source or one that seems to confuse students. In either case, we should lead students through a careful analysis of the source, modeling the practices they should employ, and helping them "decode" unfamiliar language, references, or symbols. The National Archives and Records Administration (NARA) website offers templates for analyzing various sources, from written documents to photographs and cartoons.[6]

Even with careful attention to analyzing sources, students may dismiss some perspectives represented in their archives as "stupid" and so miss important information related to their inquiry. This is particularly likely with younger students.[7] One teacher decided to try a bit of role-play to help his students understand how various perspectives related to each other. He assigned different roles and accompanying sources to some of his students, explaining that they would be responsible for helping other students—acting as class historians and newspaper reporters—understand disputes over eminent domain in their community. He divided the rest of the class into two groups: historians planning a U.S. history textbook and newspaper reporters covering the story of how a public works project would influence their community. During the next day's "interviews," the teacher had to stop several times to ask if a student was "in character"—true to the times in which he or she lived, not to today's sensibilities. Afterwards, the class discussed how the historian's reports might differ from the newspaper reports, or how one participant's diary entry might conflict with another's, and why different perspectives helped explain the controversies surrounding "preservation" and "development" efforts in their community.

Once students become comfortable with using different types of sources and with perspective recognition, they are much better prepared to search out and use sources beyond the initial archives, including:

ORAL HISTORY. Sometimes students can locate and interview people who participated in historic events or recall important information about an issue. In a community with a growing immigrant population, for instance, students interviewed people about their experiences as new arrivals in the United States. One community member recalled struggling to understand the local dialect, especially during telephone calls from her son's school. Another described his first day in the United States—hungry after a long flight, he headed for a fast food restaurant, ordered a burger and fries, but could not understand what "here or to go" meant, so fled the restaurant in confusion. As students collect accounts such as this one, they can identify a pattern of miscommunications and misunderstandings as immigrants negotiate their new community. These interviews can figure prominently in their later deliberations about ways they might help new immigrants in their school. For more on conducting oral histories with diverse populations, see Andrew Turner's *Access to History: Curriculum Planning and Practical Activities for Children with Learning Difficulties.*[8] David Ritchie's *Doing Oral History*, although intended for historians, provides helpful suggestions that can be adapted for use in classrooms.[9]

ONLINE HISTORY. A rich array of online sources can support historical inquiry. In their study of immigration, for instance, students accessed census data[10] illustrating immigration patterns over time, changing restrictions on immigration, points of entry, journal entries, pictures of different groups of immigrants, and patterns of settlement. These sources allowed them to think about the ways their local situation parallels (or differs from) national patterns. Their discovery of political cartoons about immigration led them to wonder if the local paper had ever taken a stand on immigration issues. In this instance, the information is not online, but a local editorial cartoonist can come to class and share a sample of immigration cartoons from the newspaper's archives. He could also talk to the students about the changing role of cartoons, editorials, and newspapers in regard to immigration in their community. Students could then return to online sources, including the Ellis Island site,[11] the Immigration History Research Center at the University of Minnesota,[12] Digital History,[13] National Archives,[14] the Smithsonian Asian Pacific American Program,[15] American Memory at the Library of Congress site,[16] and their state historical society's website. In a case like this, we still need to think ahead and identify appropriate sites. There are, for instance, anti-immigration sites that offer virulently hostile and factually inaccurate representations of immigration and immigrants. Providing a list of approved sites for student research guards against some of this, as do blocks on school computers, but students may still access objectionable material, and we may have to help them evaluate these sources.

LOCAL HISTORICAL REPOSITORIES. Local newspapers generally archive past issues, and local libraries and historical societies may also keep newspaper archives. While not all communities maintain historical societies, there's usually someone who stores up local history. In one school, students interested in improving recreational opportunities found several sources, including the school library, where old yearbooks and photographs documented previous forms of recreation. A local company—the major employer in the town—provided company newsletters that reported on inter-company competitions in baseball, the construction of a company-sponsored swimming pool, and the like. Another community member shared her collection of memorabilia from her time as a competitive swimmer. Someone else had stored away photographs and other documents related to the county fair, including information on horseracing and 4-H activities. In small communities, it doesn't take much searching to find these people—one good lead connects you to another. In larger communities, more formal historical organizations maintain collections that document social, cultural, economic, and political activity, and many have educational outreach programs to help students investigate local history.

Matching Evidence to Interpretation

For many students, the hardest and most frustrating part of historical inquiry happens after the data is collected. Sometimes students enthusiastically dig up information, fill in data retrieval charts, put information on timelines, and perform data-based role-plays and simulations, and then barely allude to all their data in their final "report."[17] In other cases, students craft amazingly sophisticated interpretations that draw on the evidence, account for different perspectives, and discuss alternate interpretations.[18] Several of the project descriptions in this book note that students often find that matching evidence to interpretation is challenging. What makes the difference?

First of all, the better the initiating question, the better the interpretation is likely to be. If the question makes sense, is worth asking, and is rich enough to support different perspectives, students are more likely to craft evidence-based interpretations. Eighth graders studying antebellum America from women's perspectives, for instance, asked interesting questions, including whether all women thought the same way about women's rights. Because they knew that people in their own time had very different perspectives on this issue, they began looking for differences in the past, too. They compared upper class and working class perspectives, and read sources from African American and immigrant women as well. Their interpretations attended to differences, and speculated on why there were differences within, as well as between, groups.[19]

Second, when students have manageable models of what an interpretation looks like, they tend to build better interpretations in their own work. Sometimes children's and adolescent's literature provide interesting models for interpretation. Russell Freedman's *Immigrant Kids*, for instance, interprets the immigrant experience largely through the eyes of photographer-reformers.[20] Rikki Levinson's *Watch the Stars Come Out* draws on the same experiences, but uses her grandmother's immigration story and soft pastels (rather than black and white photographs) to illustrate the story.[21] In one instance, Freedman and Levinson include an image of the same scene—a child bathing in the sink of a tenement kitchen. The photographic version of the scene presents a gritty and minimally furnished room, while the pastel version softens the scene with color and elements of the grandmother's nostalgia for her childhood home. A conversation with students about which interpretation is more accurate is interesting, allowing students to think about how perspective shapes interpretation and how they might account for that in their own work. Other authors provide wonderful models of evidence supporting an interpretation. Penny Colman's books, for instance, are readable as well as evidence-based, and she has a website with additional information about her books, her background research, and how she uses evidence to support her interpretations.[22]

In addition to models of well-crafted historical interpretations, students also benefit from developing rubrics for evaluating their work. In one class, students spent most of a class period establishing the standards by which they thought their work should be judged. They debated and defined categories, discussed what "evidence-based" meant, established percentages based on each category's importance, and posted the rubric in the room for easy reference. When they turned in their final report, they had to provide an essay explaining how they addressed each element of the rubric.

In CiviConnections projects, disciplined inquiry has served a goal beyond increased skill at crafting evidence-based historical interpretations (important as that may be), or passing a test, or receiving a good grade. Instead, students engage in disciplined inquiry into historical questions for civic purposes, including benefiting the common good and alleviating suffering. Given these purposes, evidence-based interpretation takes on particular importance as the foundation of informed agency. Students' work does not end with their interpretation. Instead, their interpretation becomes grist for the mill of deliberation: How can we best use what we have learned to make a positive difference in the world?

From Disciplined Inquiry to Informed Agency

In each of the projects described in this book, teachers felt strongly about the need to engage their students in service-learning. In some cases, teachers began with a project or issue they believed was of critical importance in their communities. In others, students identified the issues they wanted to pursue, and teachers helped them accomplish their goals. While the hope is that disciplined inquiry will lead to informed agency, we take on special responsibilities to both our students and the community when we move from disciplined inquiry to

civic action. Before taking on this responsibility, ask yourself a couple of questions:

- What do you, the teacher, think and feel about the issue under investigation? What makes you think or feel this way? Is this a topic about which you can entertain multiple perspectives? All of us have "hot button" topics where we need to monitor our responses to avoid imposing a perspective, overwhelming our students with our own opinions, or intimidating them into silence or compliance.

- Can you emphasize consensus building, as well as honor dissent, in your classroom? While it may not always feel so, dissent is fundamental to democracy. The protection of citizens' right to dissent is, therefore, a core democratic principle. Unfortunately, few students learn much about dissent in either its historic or current forms, and rarely do they experience it in the context of democratic debate and deliberation. Democratic deliberation in regard to taking civic action may involve dissent. Are you prepared to help students deal with differences in opinions about, and approaches to, civic action?

- Where will your own views figure in this project? Should you tell students at the outset what your views are, so that they can allow for possible biases? Or should you not tell them, but guard against any inclinations to manipulate and propagandize? There's no easy answer, and it may depend a great deal on the age and experiences of your students.

- What purpose do you have in asking students to pursue an inquiry into a particular issue? Again, is the issue significant enough to spend precious academic time on it? And is it an appropriate topic for your students? Is it an issue of critical importance in the community? Sometimes a problem simply is not amenable to student intervention. You and your students may feel strongly, but your students may not be able to do much about it within the course of one school year.

Conclusion

Given a current problem with historical roots amenable to investigation by children or adolescents, informed agency can be a powerful outcome of disciplined inquiry. Armed with the results of their historical (and current) inquiry, students can engage in democratic deliberation—discussion aimed at choosing a course of action. We can help our students in this important pursuit through the use of discussion templates,[23] probing questions, and graphic organizers. Inquiring about local history as a precursor to engaging in effective service and social action will ensure that our students develop a usable past—a past that helps them exercise civic agency in the give and take of our pluralist democracy. 🐚

Notes

1. M. Maimonides, *A Guide for the Perplexed* (M. Friedlander, trans.) (New York: Dover Publications, 2000).

2. W. Parker, "Knowing and Doing in Democratic Citizenship Education," in *Handbook of Research in Social Studies Education*, eds. L.S. Levstik and C. Tyson (Mahwah, NJ: Erlbaum, in press).

3. *Ibid.*, 14.

4. Linda S. Levstik and Keith C. Barton, *Doing History: Investigating with Children in Elementary and Middle Schools* (Mahwah, NJ: Erlbaum, 2005).

5. *Ibid.*

6. National Archives and Records Administration, "Teaching With Documents: Lesson Plans" (2006), www.archives.gov/education/lessons.

7. Keith C. Barton and Linda S. Levstik, *Teaching History for the Common Good* (Mahwah, NJ: Erlbaum, 2004); L. S. Levstik and D. B. Smith, "'I've Never Done This Before': Building a Community of Inquiry in a Third Grade Classroom" in *Advances in Research on Teaching: Case Studies of Teaching and Learning in Elementary History*, Vol. 5, ed. J. Brophy (JAI, 1996); Bruce VanSledright, *In Search of America's Past: Learning to Read History in Elementary School* (New York: Teachers College Press, 2002).

8. Andrew Turner, *Access to History: Curriculum Planning and Practical Activities for Children with Learning Difficulties* (Glasgow: David Fulton, 2002).

9. David Ritchie, *Doing Oral History* (New York: Oxford, 2003).

10. U.S. Census (2006), www.census.gov/population.

11. Ellis Island National Historical Park (2006), www.ellisisland.org.

12. Immigration History Research Center at the University of Minnesota (2006), www.ihrc.umn.edu.

13. Digital History, www.digitalhistory.uh.edu.

14. National Archives and Records Administration (2006).

15. Smithsonian Asian Pacific American Program (2006), www.campaignadvantage.com/services/websites/archive/smithsonian.

16. Library of Congress, "American Memory" (2006), memory.loc.gov.

17. Barton and Levstik, *Teaching History for the Common Good* (2004); Levstik and Smith, *Advances in Research on Teaching: Case Studies of Teaching and Learning in Elementary History* (1996); VanSledright, *In Search of America's Past: Learning to Read History in Elementary School* (2002).

18. Barton and Levstik, *Teaching History for the Common Good* (2004); Linda Levstik and J. Groth, "'Ruled by Our Own People': Ghanaian Adolescents' Conceptions of Citizenship," *Teachers College Record* (2005).

19. Levstik and Groth, "'Ruled by Our Own People': Ghanaian Adolescents' Conceptions of Citizenship."

20. Russell Freedman, *Immigrant Kids* (New York: Puffin, 1980).

21. Rikki Levinson, *Watch the Stars Come Out* (New York: Puffin Books, 1985).

22. Penny Colman (2006), www.pennycolman.com.

23. Levstik and Barton, *Doing History* (2005), 140.

CHAPTER TWO

Community Service–Learning for Democratic Citizenship

RAHIMA C. WADE

The professed goal of social studies instruction is to create informed and active public citizens,[1] yet adults in the United States do not vote or engage in political involvement in great numbers. Many social studies scholars are deeply concerned about this fact, realizing that a democracy lacking in participation by the majority of its constituents is a democracy at risk. For a thriving democracy, we need a majority of citizens willing to participate in community life and to contribute to decisions, from the local to the international level, that affect their own lives and the common good.

To many social studies educators, service-learning as an educational activity makes sense, both for students and communities. However, some educators have questioned the potential of service-learning for developing active and informed citizens. How can service-learning in social studies courses effectively educate students for democratic citizenship? This is a question for serious deliberation, given the time, energy, and effort involved in service-learning activities. I will explore the question in this chapter; first, through a definition of democratic citizenship; second, in an analysis of the school's role in developing citizens; and third, through a discussion of the potential of service-learning as a means for civic education. Finally, I will offer the definition and essential elements of service-learning that form the basis of the CiviConnections program.

A Definition of Citizenship for a Democracy

A democracy depends on the informed and active participation of its members, not just in the political sphere, but in the life of its communities as well. In the early years of America's history, communal participation was essential, not only for democratic governance, but also for the health and well-being of each person. Citizens needed each other to build homes, grow food, and provide a wide array of other services and goods necessary for living.

From the onset of industrialization to the present, many Americans have increasingly valued independence and personal success over their commitment to a healthy, egalitarian community. While one can also point to the prevalence of volunteerism throughout American history, our society's evolution from a communal to a more individualistic focus has been well documented.[2] Barber described present-day America in stark terms as:

> ...a place where individuals regard themselves almost exclusively as private persons with responsibilities only to family and job, yet possessing endless rights against a distant and alien state in relationship to which they think of themselves at best, as watchdogs and clients, and, at worst, as adversaries and victims.[3]

In our individualistic society, some may believe that citizenship is more a matter of respecting individuals' rights than of working for the rights of others, of minding one's own business than of serving the public interest, or of obeying public laws and social norms than of questioning their inequitable nature and seeking to change them for the better. Yet the reality of a democracy necessitates the active involvement of a majority of its members. As Barber noted, "Democracy does not just 'deserve' our gratitude; it demands our participation as a price of survival."[4]

How then should we define citizenship in a democratic society? Is a "good citizen" a person who just votes in local and national elections, obeys laws, and is informed about political events? Conrad and Hedin asserted that the notion of a citizen, for most people, goes beyond political involvement to "the person who acts decently, who knows and cares about the affairs of his community, and who demonstrates this concern through overt actions."[5] Thus, being a good citizen extends beyond working in one's own best interests. In the CiviConnections program, the idea of citizenship has encompassed varied types of social participation, within the recognition that as one works for positive change in the community, one is serving a public good that is also one's own.

Citizenship and Schooling

In America's early years, the relationship between schooling and citizenship was taken for granted. Indeed, the original purpose for establishing public schooling was to develop informed, community-minded citizens. Schools are the sole institution available to society as a whole to train our youth in the theory and practice of democratic citizenship. While church, family, the media, and the streets all play powerful roles in children's development, schools provide the greatest opportunity for youth to experience community, to work toward common goals, and to uphold both individual rights and collective good.

As a public institution, the school mirrors society. Thus, the trend toward individualism so prevalent in our nation is evident in our schools as well. Often in public school classrooms, students are assigned individual seatwork, and communication is discouraged, if not forbidden. Learning is seen as a predominately individual pursuit; grades and competition foster an ethic of individual success over collective learning. While this image is certainly not true of all classrooms in the United States, it is prevalent enough to raise the types of fears confessed here by one educator:

> I am worried about the cumulative impact that ignoring others has upon the civic imagination of young people. I do not want young people to believe that to be a good citizen one must simply stay within one's own morally protected space—that space described by the idea of possession—and never to serve others or join with others. A society in which citizens always stand at a distance from each other because they fear that joining might violate someone's right of possession would not be a decent society. Yet I have reason to believe that is precisely how students perceive citizenship in our nation's classrooms.[6]

Clearly, the social relationships in schools teach our youth as much, if not more, about citizenship than the lessons in their social studies textbooks. As educators, therefore, we must be mindful of how we organize our classrooms, how we encourage or discourage collaboration among students, and how we incorporate opportunities for meaningful involvement both in the school and the community.

Service-Learning as a Means for Civic Education

Through both content and process, service-learning incorporates an ethic of democratic citizenship. It is not enough to just talk about democratic ideals in our social studies classes or even to practice them within the classroom setting alone. If we want students to develop the skills and values necessary for effective involvement in their communities, then we must provide them with opportunities to learn these skills and values experientially. "The ultimate training ground for civic competence is engagement in the resolution of the issues and problems that confront our society. It is an evasion of our responsibility as educators to stop short of this engagement."[7]

Within the diversity of opportunities for youth participation in service-learning, students should be able to perform tasks that are worthwhile for both the students and the community, be able to make some significant decisions, have others depend on their actions, work on tasks that challenge their thinking, work with peers and adults on group efforts toward common goals, and reflect systematically on their experience.[8] Additionally, the focus of students' service-learning efforts should be on significant social, political, or environmental issues.

Service-learning as a part of educating for democratic citizenship makes sense for at least four reasons. First, it can break down barriers between institutions and groups in the community. Schools and public agencies can work toward common goals that meet both educational objectives and community needs. Second, service-learning can give students the experience of truly making a difference to someone, an experience that may be necessary in developing the sense of personal efficacy that one must have to believe that it is worthwhile to try to change anything in society. Third, putting students in positions of responsibility may lead them to develop or discover the skills they need for many other types of civic participation. Finally, service-learning can provide an application and illustration of classroom learning about citizenship, firsthand experience with various means and institutions for dealing with social problems, a feeling of caring for others, and an issue to care about—thus serving as an impetus to work for future changes in social policy.[9]

The discipline of social studies is especially well situated to play a major role in the growing service-learning movement. Although social studies educators differ in their views about what constitutes citizenship,[10] many have asserted that an essential component of civic education is students' active involvement in the social and political life of the community.[11] Moreover, the history of social studies education reveals a legacy of service and community activism,[12] from the early work of Arthur Dunn and the 1916 Social Studies Committee through numerous National Council for the Social Studies publications,[13] including the recent position statement, "Service-Learning: An Essential Component of Citizenship Education."[14]

Having established the importance of service-learning to the civic mission of social studies, we now examine a definition of service-learning and a discussion of the essential elements of service-learning practice at the heart of the CiviConnections program.

Service-Learning Defined

Service-learning programs can take a variety of shapes and forms, making the defining of service-learning a challenging task. Differences in definition reflect various opinions about the nature of service-learning (philosophy of education, curricular strategy, or program design) and its purpose (e.g., personal growth, social skills development, or civic competence).[15] In recognition of the need for a widely agreed-upon definition of service-learning and a set of standards by which to judge programs, a diverse national group of service-learning educators—the Alliance for Service-Learning in Education Reform (ASLER)—established the following definition. While differences of opinion still persist, this definition is widely used:

> Service-learning is a method by which young people learn and develop through active participation in thoughtfully organized service experiences that meet actual community needs; that are coordinated in collaboration with the school and community; that are integrated into each young person's academic curriculum; that provide structured time for a young person to think, talk, and write about what he/she did and saw during the actual service activity; that provide young people with opportunities to use newly acquired academic skills and knowledge in real life situations in their own communities; that enhance what is taught in the school by extending student learning beyond the classroom; and that help to foster the development of a sense of caring for others.[16]

The components of curriculum integration and reflection are, in fact, what distinguishes service-learning from community service. Service-learning is not an isolated activity; it is a pedagogical method in which service projects form the basis of learning opportunities. Service-learning is based on a vision of youth as capable, productive, and essential contributors to their communities. High quality service-learning programs include all of the following essential elements: thoughtful preparation, respectful collaboration, meaningful service, curriculum integration, structured reflection activities, evaluation of service and learning, student ownership, and community celebration.[17]

While in almost all cases, service-learning projects have a goal of promoting active citizenship (and thus could be thought of as enhancing the goal of social studies), social studies educators can develop activities especially suited to their curricula. For example, elementary students could study the historical buildings in their community and work on restoring one site. High school students might conduct a voter registration drive, making presentations to groups that are typically underrepresented in the voter pool. As part of a unit on immigration, middle school students could interview recent immigrants in their community and take care of young children while their parents study for their U.S. citizenship tests. In all of these projects, the service experience becomes the motivation and central activity for connecting social studies knowledge, attitudes, and civic skills and behaviors.

Essential Elements of Quality Service-Learning

The ASLER definition previously cited lists many of the essential elements of quality service-learning programs. Additional sources, for more detailed discussion than can be provided here, include: *Principles of Combining Service and Learning;*[18] *Service-Learning: Core Elements;*[19] and *Community Service-Learning: A Guide to Including Service in the Public School Curriculum.*[20] Seven central elements for quality service-learning programs are addressed briefly here: preparation, collaboration, service, curriculum integration, reflection, celebration, and evaluation. (Much of the rest of this chapter is excerpted from a previous National Council for the Social Studies Bulletin, *Building Bridges: Connecting Classroom and Community through Service-Learning in Social Studies.*[21] Please refer to this publication for more research and numerous examples of social studies-based service-learning practice in K-12 and teacher education).

Preparation

Planning and preparing for a service-learning project is a critical step in fostering success. There are many ways to begin planning a project. Some social studies teachers start with their curricular goals and consider what types of service experiences will enhance course content and skills. Others, particularly at the elementary level, develop the service activity first and then create curriculum connections with social studies and other subject areas, such as language arts and math. With all projects, it is wise to begin by considering parameters for the scope of the experience. How much time do you want to devote to the service and reflection activities? Are there funds and transportation to support an out-of-school experience or would it be better to focus on a school-based need or problem? What community agencies are within walking distance of the school? Is there a particular issue that is of concern to you, your students, and/or the community? What types of service activities easily connect with your curricular goals?

Teachers should be sure to include all stakeholders in the planning of the project. Students and community agency members should have a say in how the project unfolds. Informing parents and administrators during the planning stage can help to address any concerns and potentially lead to additional resources and supporters. Are there other faculty or staff in the school that might work with you on this project?

Considering the logistical aspects of your service-learning project during the preparation stage may thwart potential problems down the road. Consider issues such as scheduling, transportation, and liability for off-campus activities. If your project will need funding, brainstorm possible avenues for acquiring this support. Will you need additional adults to help supervise students in the community? Oftentimes students can be especially helpful in coming up with ideas to address the logistical aspects of the project.

Orientation is another key activity during the planning phase. If students are going out into the community to work with others or help out at a community agency, they need to be prepared for this experience. Likewise, if the agency is new to student volunteers, it may be helpful to orient agency members in regard to their expectations of the students.

Finally, think about the learning component of your project during this early stage. How will you ensure that students connect their experience with the course content? In what ways and how often will you have students reflect on their experiences in the community? How will you evaluate student learning? Planning ahead will ensure that your project is a success, both in the community and in the classroom.

Collaboration

Service-learning projects generally involve several types of collaboration. First, it is likely that students will work together in small or large groups to carry out various aspects of the project. They may also be working directly with others in the community, perhaps serving senior citizens, preschoolers, or individuals with economic or health needs. Often the individu-

als with whom they are working are different from themselves culturally or in other significant ways. Do your students have the skills for these varied types of collaborations? If not, which civic education skills will it be important to teach them in the classroom? Some possibilities include interview skills, conflict resolution strategies, or decision-making techniques. Minkler identified several democratic skills that students may employ in conducting service-learning projects: respectful deliberation and dialogue, coalition building, developing creative solutions that meet everyone's needs, and gathering support from a broad audience in the community.[22]

As the teacher, it is likely that you will be collaborating with others with whom you have not been involved before. Think about who might be potential collaborators in your school, neighborhood, and local community. If you are approaching a particular community agency about a possible collaboration, be sure to consider the agency's point of view. Rather than propose a specific project, ask the agency director what needs or problems the agency is most concerned with at this time. Then brainstorm project possibilities with your students and agency members to develop a plan that is mutually beneficial for all involved.

It is important to note that collaborations with community members are likely to change over time. Initial enthusiasm can lessen if a project is not conducted with care. Agencies may be cautious about taking on student volunteers if they have not previously done so. In a successful service-learning project, community members will come to value the services your students provide and continue to invest the agency's time and resources toward your collaboration.

Service

True service is more than an action; it is an attitude, a relationship, and a way of being in the world. There are numerous types of service projects suitable for the social studies curriculum. While the following categories are somewhat arbitrary, service experiences can be labeled as either direct, indirect, or advocacy activities.

Direct service involves working with others in the school or community, or hands-on involvement with animals or the environment. Students may work with senior citizens, younger children, individuals who are learning English as a second language, people with disabilities or illnesses, or people living in poverty. Whenever possible, individuals from these groups should be included in the planning phase of the project to ensure that the activities will be mutually beneficial for all involved. The best service-learning projects ensure that all individuals involved are contributing their skills, talents, and interests toward making the community a better place for everyone. Students can sometimes develop condescending attitudes toward those they are helping and may need to be reminded that service-learning should be about solidarity, not charity.

Indirect service activities are fund-raisers or collection programs that generate money or resources that can be contributed to an organization working on a community problem. While indirect service activities are generally easier to coordinate because they can be completed at school, teachers should consider the value of students working directly with others as well. Following are just a few of the ways students and teachers can fund raise for a worthy cause:

  Passing the hat at a meeting
  Canvassing door-to-door or by telephone
  Holding a dance
  Sponsoring a performance or concert
  Screening a movie
  Sponsoring a walk-a-thon, work-a-thon, or road race
  Creating a newspaper ad
  Organizing a festival or carnival
  Selling t-shirts, bumper stickers, or buttons
  Holding a raffle
  Having a bake sale or yard sale
  Coordinating a car wash

Students can organize school-wide collections of the following items: canned food, newspapers and other recyclables, animal shelter supplies (food, toys, etc.), clothing, books, infant items (disposable diapers, formula, baby food, etc.), or personal hygiene supplies (toothpaste, soap, shampoo, etc.). A third type of indirect service project is an adoption program where students pay for the preservation of rainforest acreage or endangered species.

Perhaps the most useful types of service-learning experiences for social studies educators concerned with developing students' civic participation skills are advocacy activities. The following activities give students opportunities to share what they have learned with others in the community, to work for community improvement through social and political channels, and to learn a variety of methods for public communication. Most of these activities are more suitable for secondary students, though several could be adapted for the elementary level. Advocacy activities include:

  Creating public displays
  Offering public performances

  Writing editorials
  Making public service announcements
  Lobbying public officials
  Developing and distributing pamphlets, leaflets, or flyers
  Speaking at public meetings
  Phoning public officials
  Writing letters to public officials
  Writing a newsletter
  Developing a speaker's bureau
  Setting up a public hearing
  Boycotting products or businesses
  Organizing a demonstration or protest
  Writing a news release
  Participating in a call-in radio show
  Writing a grant
  Circulating a petition
  Proposing a bill for a new law
  Being a youth representative on a local board or city council
  Campaigning for an issue, ballot item, or candidate
  Planning a news conference
  Making and putting up posters
  Conducting a survey or public opinion poll, and publicizing
      the results
  Setting up a telephone hot line
  Holding a contest
  Developing and distributing awards
  Developing a program for public access TV
  Setting up a web page or listserv

While all of these activities provide valuable learning opportunities for young citizens, they take time to plan and carry out. Sometimes social studies teachers are concerned that the time spent on service will take away from covering course content. While teachers of older students sometimes counter this problem by having them complete service activities during out-of-school time, there are several facts it is important to keep in mind here. First, students rarely remember for very long information they don't use. Would you rather your students memorized thirty facts for a test this week and forget almost all of them two weeks later, or would you rather that your students learned ten facts and retained the information, because they used these ideas and experienced how they apply to civic life? Service experiences not only enhance the application of classroom knowledge, but in addition, students' motivation to learn social studies content increases when they realize that they can use their book knowledge to make a difference in their school or community.

Curriculum Integration

Curriculum integration is what distinguishes a valuable service-learning project from a useful community service activity. Thus, it is essential that the project be connected with academic skills and content. Many resources are available to assist social studies educators in brainstorming the ways service can enhance the curriculum.

At the elementary level, teachers often integrate service-learning into a variety of subject areas. For example, a fourth grade classroom studying cultures around the world might read books about different types of bread and their origins, and then use their math skills to bake several types of bread for the local soup kitchen. A third grade curriculum on communities presents numerous opportunities for service activities. Fifth graders studying U.S. history might identify several grassroots movements that have contributed to change in our country (e.g., civil rights, the women's movement, or animal rights) and then choose one with which to get involved. All of these projects could easily incorporate students developing their reading and writing skills.

At the secondary level, when the social studies curriculum becomes more content-oriented, matching the service activity with the curriculum becomes an even more important task. In the CiviConnections program, middle and high school teachers effectively matched community issues of concern and interest to their students with their curricular goals and content.

Reflection

Reflection is a means for reliving or recapturing our experience in order to make sense of it, to learn from it, and to develop new understandings and appreciation. Reflection takes place throughout a quality service-learning project, not just at the end of the experience. Critical to students' willingness to reflect honestly and deeply is a classroom climate based on mutual respect, caring, and openness to divergent ideas. At the beginning of a service-learning project, encourage students to reflect on their assumptions, stereotypes, fears, desires, and other preconceived notions. During the time period students are engaged in service, they should focus on processing their feelings and experiences, and developing approaches to address challenges they are facing. The end of the service-learning activity is the best time for students to draw conclusions about their experience, to connect what they have learned from their experience with course goals and content, and to apply their knowledge to thinking about future civic involvement.

There are numerous ways to have students reflect in a service-learning project. Often teachers will encourage students to journal about their experiences; discussion is also a frequently used method. Students will gain more from the reflection process when teachers structure the reflection activity to focus on specific aspects of their experience. For example, in addition to journaling or discussing what happened at the service site, what problems were encountered, or how students felt, social studies teachers can foster students' learning by asking questions such as "What civic participation skills did you use during this project?" or "How did your experiences working with others in the community support or challenge what we learned about in the textbook?" Following are several questions teachers can use to help students reflect on a societal issue central to their service-learning project and the notion of citizenship generally.

Societal Issues

- What new knowledge have you learned about this issue through your service experience?
- What human needs or problems are created by this issue?
- How are individuals and groups in the community (nation, world) attempting to address this issue?
- What historical events have been connected with this issue?
- What are the current political, economic, and social contexts influencing this issue?
- In your opinion, what are the best approaches to try to create positive change concerning this issue?

Citizenship

- What is a good citizen?
- What type of citizen do you think you will be when you grow up?
- What are the ways that citizens help their communities?
- How does a democracy depend on civic participation?
- What would happen in our democracy if everyone participated in public life?
- What would happen in our democracy if only a few individuals participated in public life?
- Is community service an essential component of good citizenship in a democracy? Why or why not?

In addition to journaling and discussion, there are many other useful means for fostering students' reflections on their service experiences. They include creative writing, writing persuasive letters, concept mapping, writing a guide for future program participants, creating artistic expressions (theatre, music, dance, visual arts), developing a school-wide or community display, and presenting at a public meeting or conference. Many of these activities can also be used as a means for evaluating students' learning.

Celebration

Celebrating students' service-learning efforts is not just a way to have fun at the end of the project. Celebration also serves a variety of other goals: publicizing the project, saying "thank you" to those who helped, developing new support for the program, and honoring and renewing the commitment of those who will continue to be involved. Celebrations can range from small student-only popcorn parties to large public events open to the entire community. Students should be encouraged to help plan the event and to think about ways that they can share the results of their efforts (e.g., photo display, video, slide show, or awards presentations). Of course, food is a must. Be sure to offer some healthy, vegetarian, and/or wheat-free items for those individuals who may be on restricted diets. Celebrations that bring together most or all of a project's participants can help everyone see the impact that the program has had on the community.

Evaluation

Evaluation in a service-learning program serves several purposes. First, it is important to assess what students have learned from the experience. Was the chosen service activity effective in enhancing the course content and goals? Are students aware of the civic participation skills they used or developed during the project? What are students' views about the community impact of their efforts? In general, did they believe their efforts were successful? Do they plan on continuing to volunteer or participate in civic life in other ways? Social studies teachers can answer these questions through a variety of methods, including tests, essays, writing assignments, individual interviews, or analysis of students' journals.

A second purpose of evaluation is to make modifications in the program. Distributing a brief survey or conducting phone interviews with project participants in the school or community can assist the process of improving the project. While surveys are perhaps the easiest means for collecting responses to the same questions from many individuals, phone or personal interviews may net more in-depth information or ideas that weren't even inquired about.

Sometimes teachers will need to collect evaluation data to provide to funding sources (as with a state or federal grant) or to justify continuation of the project to administrators. Some of the information needed can be gleaned from the evaluation measures described above. However, often the most impressive data for these audiences involves numbers of participants, hours spent on service, funds spent, funds saved by the agency due to students' efforts, and so forth. If you know you will need to compile this data by the end of the project, develop a system in the beginning for doing so. Students can keep track of their efforts via timesheets and agency members can be informed ahead of time about information that will be requested.

Conclusion

Service-learning is an especially suitable strategy for the social studies, given the profession's mission of creating active and informed citizens. Teachers' success in conducting quality service-learning projects will be enhanced if they collaborate with students, school personnel, and community members; match service activities to course goals and content; and provide frequent and varied opportunities for students to reflect on their experience. Through thoughtfully structured service-learning projects, social studies teachers can provide their students with opportunities to develop their civic participation skills and attitudes, while working on problems of concern in the community. The CiviConnections program has provided one effective model for service-learning that integrates social studies subject matter with community service and social action. 🖎

Notes

1. R. D. Barr, J. L. Barth and S. S. Shermis, *Defining the Social Studies* (Washington, DC: National Council for the Social Studies, 1977); National Council for the Social Studies, "Revision of the National Council for the Social Studies Curriculum Guidelines," *Social Education* 43 (1977): 261-273; W. Parker, "Participatory Citizenship: Civics in the Strong Sense," *Social Education* 53 (1989): 353-354; J. P. Shaver, ed., *Building Rationales for Citizenship Education* (Washington, DC: National Council for the Social Studies, 1977).

2. B. Barber, *An Aristocracy of Everyone: The Politics of Education and the Future of America* (NY: Ballantine Books, 1992); Robert Bellah, et al., *Habits of the Heart* (Berkeley: University of California Press, 1985).

3. Barber, 232.

4. *Ibid.*, 260.

5. Dan Conrad and Diane Hedin, "Citizenship Education through Participation," in *Education for Responsible Citizenship: The Report of the National Task Force on Citizenship Education*, ed. B. F. Brown (New York: McGraw-Hill, 1977), 133-156.

6. D. C. Bricker, *Classroom Life as Civic Education: Individual Achievement and Student Cooperation in Schools* (New York: Teachers College Press, 1989).

7. Shirley Engle and Anna Ochoa, *Education for Democratic Citizenship: Decision Making in the Social Studies* (New York: Teachers College Press, 1988).

8. Conrad and Hedin, "Citizenship Education through Participation," (1977).

9. *Ibid.*

10. S. Shermis and J. Barth, "Teaching for Passive Citizenship: A Critique of Philosophical Assumptions," *Theory and Research in Social Education* 10, (1982): 17-37.

11. Engle and Ochoa, *Education for Democratic Citizenship: Decision Making in the Social Studies* (1988); Janet Eyler and Dwight Giles, Jr., *Where's the Learning in Service-Learning?* (San Francisco: Jossey-Bass, 1999); Walter Parker and John Jarolimek, *Citizenship and the Critical Role of the Social Studies* (Washington, DC: National Council for the Social Studies, 1984); Richard Pratte, *The Civic Imperative: Examining the Need for Civic Education* (New York: Teachers College Press, 1988); R. A. Rutter and F. M. Newmann, "The Potential of Community Service to Enhance Civic Responsibility," *Social Education* 53, no. 6 (October 1989): 371-374; M. C. Schug and R. Beery, *Community Study: Applications and Opportunities* (Washington, DC: National Council for the Social Studies, 1984).

12. Rahima C. Wade and David Warren Saxe, "Community Service-Learning in the Social Studies: Historical Roots, Empirical Evidence, Critical Issues," *Theory and Research in Social Education* 24, no. 4 (Fall 1996): 331-359.

13. National Council for the Social Studies, "Revision of the National Council for the Social Studies Curriculum Guidelines," *Social Education* 43, no. 4 (April 1979): 261-273; National Council for the Social Studies, *National Council for the Social Studies Essentials of Social Studies* (Washington, DC: National Council for the Social Studies, 1980); National Council for the Social Studies, *Social Studies for Citizens of a Strong and Free Nation – Report of the National Council for the Social Studies Task Force on Scope and Sequence* (Washington, DC: National Council for the Social Studies, 1989); National Council for the Social Studies, *Expectations of Excellence: Curriculum Standards for Social Studies* (Washington, DC: National Council for the Social Studies, 1994).

14. National Council for the Social Studies, "Service-Learning: An Essential Component of Citizenship Education," *Social Education* 65, no. 4 (May-June 2001): 240-241.

15. Shelley Billig, "Research on K-12 School-Based Service-Learning: The Evidence Builds," *Phi Delta Kappan* 81 (2000): 658-664.

16. Alliance for Service-Learning in Education Reform, *Standards of Quality For School-Based Service-Learning* (Chester, VT: Alliance for Service-Learning in Education Reform, 1993).

17. Alliance for Service-Learning in Education Reform, *Standards of Quality For School-Based Service-Learning* (1993); Billig, *Research on K-12 School-Based Service-Learning: The Evidence Builds* (2000); Dan Conrad and Diane Hedin, "School-Based Community Service: What We Know from Research and Theory," *Phi Delta Kappan* 72, no. 10 (1991): 743-749; D. Giles, E. P. Honnet, and S. Migliore, *Research Agenda for Combining Service and Learning in the 1990s* (Raleigh, NC: National Society for Experiential Education, 1991).

18. Giles, Honnet, and Migliore, *Research Agenda for Combining Service and Learning in the 1990s* (1991).

19. Mark Langseth, "Service-Learning: Core Elements," *The Generator* 10, (Spring 1990): 6.

20. Rahima Wade, ed., *Community Service-Learning: A Guide to Including Service in the Public School Curriculum* (Albany, NY: State University of New York Press, 1997).

21. Rahima Wade, ed., *Building Bridges: Connecting Classroom and Community through Service-Learning in Social Studies* (Washington, DC: National Council for the Social Studies, 2000).

22. John Minkler, "Service Learning," in *The American Promise Teaching Guide* (Los Angeles: Farmers Insurance Group, 1996), 151-185.

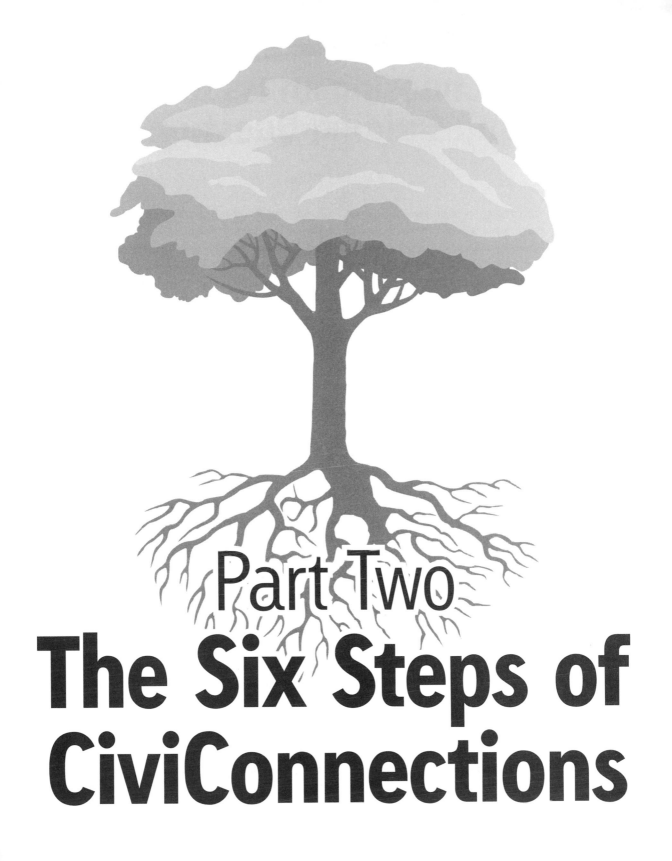

Part Two
The Six Steps of CiviConnections

CHAPTER THREE

Choosing an Issue and Guiding Question

RAHIMA C. WADE

The first step in the CiviConnections program has been to choose a social or environmental issue as a focus for learning and service, and developing a guiding question for the inquiry to follow. This chapter provides multiple avenues for you and your students to choose an issue, and also offers a list of issues relevant for many communities, and guidelines on developing a guiding question.

Pathways to Choosing an Issue

There are many different strategies teachers and students can use to choose a community issue as a focus for a project like those of CiviConnections. Here are some of the possibilities.

1. Begin with the curriculum.

Look at your curriculum content, standards, and goals. What issue does the curriculum address that is also central to your community? Are there skills or values central to your social studies curriculum that could best be taught through a particular issue? For which issue are you most likely to find helpful curricular resources? (Resources can include websites, news articles, children's literature books, etc.)

2. Begin with something of interest.

What issue is likely to be of most interest to your students? What issue have you as a teacher been involved with in your community? Is there an issue that promises to be of greater interest to parents and community members who might assist with your project?

3. Begin with the community.

Look at newspapers or talk to members of the community. What issues are of particular interest to your community? Which present multiple opportunities for problem solving and action?

Selection of a suitable issue may be the most important part of your project. Skeel suggests the following questions to guide a teacher's choice of an issue to study in the classroom.[1]

1. Is the issue of real significance?
2. Is it likely to be, or has it been, continually recurring?
3. Will the students become better-informed, thoughtful citizens as a result of the study?
4. Does the issue require judgment and/or critical thinking?
5. Are the children sufficiently mature and experienced to thoroughly understand the study?
6. Is it appropriate for the children's developmental level?

When considering the choice of an issue as a focus for a project, the following additional questions may be helpful to consider:

1. Is this issue one that can readily be connected to the required curriculum content, skills, and standards?
2. Are there opportunities to connect this issue to meaningful and needed service to the local community?
3. Is this an issue that is likely to engender widespread interest among students, parents, and community members?
4. Will student involvement with this issue likely lead to increased civic attitudes and values, and future civic action?

Who Decides?

An important consideration is: Who will decide on the community issue? You? Your students? Both of you together? There are advantages and drawbacks in each situation. For example, if you choose the issue, there may be greater opportunities for curriculum integration, and much groundwork in planning and gathering resources can be completed in the summer before school begins in the fall. However, students may not feel ownership of the project and some may lack interest in participating. If the students decide on the issue, they may choose one that is difficult to connect to curricular goals and standards, or one that may not be significant in the local community. Perhaps the best approach is for both you and your students to have some input into the choice of a community issue. This can be accomplished in many ways. Here are several possibilities:

1. You choose a broad category and your students choose an issue within that category.

This approach allows you to choose an area of concern that is central to the community and can be readily connected with the curriculum. At the same time, your students have some ownership of the project, as they brainstorm and vote on, or come to, consensus on an issue. For example, you might choose "safety" as a broad category and your students might brainstorm the following list from which to choose one issue: disaster preparedness, hate crimes, violence, teen crime, gangs, gun control, and drug/alcohol abuse.

2. Students brainstorm a list of possibilities based on given criteria.

Students consider the variety of issues that are problems in their community. Each issue in the list is evaluated according to the following criteria: significance to the community, connection with the required curriculum, opportunities for meaningful service and action, interest to students, and interest to others in the community.

3. Students gather suggestions from parents and community members, present viable issues to the class and vote on three. Then you select one of the three issues.

This process also allows for community input. The disadvantage to this strategy may be the time involved: surveying others, planning and presenting their ideas, and voting on the top three will take a week or more of class time. On the other hand, students have some input, yet you can choose the issue that is of the greatest significance and/or is most readily connected to the curriculum.

Possible Issues for CiviConnections Projects

Regardless of the strategies used to decide on an issue, there are likely to be many possible and suitable community issues in any location. Think about your community as you consider the following list of social and environmental issues:

Hunger/Malnutrition	Graffiti	High School Dropouts
Homelessness	Voter Apathy	Teen Pregnancy
Racism/Prejudice/Hate Crimes/ Racial Profiling/Stereotyping	Unemployment/Jobs	Food Additives
Poverty	Literacy	Pesticides
Child Abuse	Conservation/Endangered Species/ Wildlife Rescue and Rehabilitation/ Habitat Destruction	False Advertising
AIDS		Public Transportation
Mental Illness	Lead-based Paint	Child Labor
Disabilities	Loneliness	Prostitution
Immigration	Healthcare	Eating Disorders
Gangs	Substance Abuse/Smoking/ Alcoholism	Acid Rain
School Violence		Global Warming
Pollution/Toxic Waste/ Trash/Litter	Bicycle Safety	Sexism
Safety/Crime	Landfills	Anti-Semitism
Gun Control	Pets	Homophobia
Human Rights	Water Quality	Single Mothers
	Air Quality	Disaster Preparedness
	Elderly	

a few of the many issues that beset our society. ...issue selected should be of critical importance ..., provide opportunities for meaningful con-...urriculum, and be both interesting to, and ...ror, your students.

Developing a Guiding Question

Once an issue is selected, the next step is for you and your students to develop one or more guiding questions. As Levstik noted in Chapter 1 of this book, interesting and challenging historical questions will serve both to guide an effective inquiry and inform a meaningful service-learning activity. Suitable questions are open-ended, invite multiple perspectives, and help students compare the past with the present. They are worthwhile questions that lead to meaningful curricular connections, students' development of important skills and knowledge, and ideas for student-appropriate civic engagement and service. Consider again the following examples of issues and related guiding questions from Chapter 1:

> VOTER APATHY – How has who votes changed over time? Are people more likely to vote in local elections now or in the past?

> IMMIGRATION – How have Americans responded to immigration in the past? Why are southern border crossings more controversial than crossings along our northern border?

NATURAL DISASTER RELIEF – How have communities dealt with natural disasters in the past? What responses have been effective in our community?

Note that one cannot simply answer "yes" or "no" to these questions, nor can they be resolved with one simple explanation. To answer these questions, students will need to collect a variety of data to best determine their next steps to making a difference in their community.

Conclusion

There are many criteria that figure into the selection of a suitable issue to investigate: interest, developmental appropriateness, available resources, potential for curriculum connections, and opportunities for service, to name a few. Once a community issue has been selected, you and your students can then frame the upcoming inquiry with one or more guiding questions. Then the class will be ready to begin the process of learning about this issue in their community's history. In Chapter 4, we discuss the strategies and resources for engaging students in local historical inquiry.

Note

1. Dorothy Skeel, "An Issues-Centered Elementary Curriculum," in *Handbook on Teaching Social Issues*, eds. R. W. Evans and D. W. Saxe (Washington, D.C.: National Council for the Social Studies, 1996), 230-236.

CHAPTER FOUR

Investigating Our Community's History

RAHIMA C. WADE

This chapter offers a range of strategies for involving students in learning about their chosen issue in the local community's history. Students are encouraged to engage in firsthand research as they talk to longtime residents of the community, as well as to access the community's written records.

Developing a Community Investigation Plan

After the issue and guiding question(s) are selected, the next part of the project is to learn about the issue in the local community's history. Teachers and students can develop a plan together and then divide up the tasks for individuals, pairs, or small groups of students to carry out. There are two primary data collection strategies students will use in their firsthand research: interviewing and document analysis.

Interviewing

As a class, talk about who in the community might know about the selected issue. These individuals might include: longtime residents of the community, people affected by the issue, people working in businesses or social service agencies that address the issue, and local community historians, among others.

For example, if the chosen issue is homelessness, students might want to interview senior citizens who have been longtime residents of the community; homeless or formerly homeless individuals; and people who work at the local homeless shelter, food bank, or free medical clinic. In addition, students might want to talk to employees at the unemployment office, and a community historian at the county historical society.

After a list of potential interviewees is established, these individuals should be contacted to request their time and interest in an interview. A brief letter or e-mail invitation in advance of a phone call will give the people contacted by you or your students time to think about whether they would be interested in participating or not. Interviews could be conducted over the phone or in person, during class time or as homework. Another

option would be to mail or e-mail the interview questions to the individual, and ask them to respond in writing. In an elementary classroom, teachers might want to invite several interviewees to come to school for a panel-type interview. An invitation to participate might look something like this:

September 8, 2007

Dear _____;

   Mr. Smith's 8th grade social studies class is learning about homelessness in our community's history in an effort to determine how we can help. We would like to interview you to learn what you know about homelessness in our community.

   Someone from our class will call you to see if you would be willing to participate in a phone or in-person interview sometime in the next two weeks. We look forward to learning from you. If you have any questions about our class project, you can e-mail Mr. Smith at rrsmith@aol.com.

Sincerely,
Mr. Smith's class

   While some students are writing or typing letters and mailing them, others can be brainstorming what questions interviewees should be asked. Here are some possible questions, again focused on the theme of homelessness:

- How does your job or your life experience in our community inform you about homelessness?
- Do you think homelessness is a major problem in our community? If yes, why? If no, why not?
- Can you trace the history of homelessness in our community? If yes, when did the problem begin? What caused it? What have people tried to do to help solve this problem?
- Do you have or know of any written information that

would help us understand the history of homelessness in our community?

- What strategies are being used now to try to solve the problem of homelessness? Who is involved? What agencies or businesses are working on this problem?
- Which strategies do you think are most effective? Why?
- Do you have any ideas for strategies that could be tried in the future?
- Who else do you think we should interview to learn more about homelessness?

This last question is an important one, as it may result in additional interviewees for the project. While students should be free to ask additional questions of interest or relevance to the particular interview they are conducting, having everyone use a standard set of interview questions will greatly assist students with assembling their information and drawing conclusions from the data collected.

As students conduct their interviews, they can either tape record and then transcribe the interviewee's comments, or just take notes. A class discussion focused on the interview questions one at a time will allow students to share what they learned and come to some conclusions. It is likely that there will be conflicting information and viewpoints gathered. This is a valuable lesson for students to learn—that history is not just one specific set of facts, but rather that there are always multiple perspectives of any given situation or event. Thus, it is not necessary to resolve or try to find the "truth" with every aspect of the issue. However, examining written documents and information may aid students in coming to more defensible conclusions about the issue under study.

Examining Written Documents

Students should ask about available written information during their interviews, as well as seek out any of the following print resources they think may be helpful:

- Newspaper archives (for past news articles and letters to the Editor)
- Community agency documents and websites (for letters, policies, and other documents on the issue)

- Historical society documents (for primary sources, e.g., old photos relevant to the issue)
- Local television or radio archives (for past TV or radio shows on the issue)
- Local public library (for agency brochures and other locally written publications)
- Local city council archives (for meeting minutes or transcriptions where the issue was discussed or legislation passed on the issue)

As much as possible, empower students to be the ones who make phone calls, write e-mails or letters, or go to businesses and agencies to find out about print resources. With elementary school children, you may want to take more of a leadership role in seeking out and even obtaining resources. However, these should be shared with the class, and students of all ages should then discuss what they have learned and how this information affirms or conflicts with the information they gathered in their interviews.

Writing a Community History

Once students have completed their community investigation, they can write a community history of the selected issue, using interview and print resources to document their views. Community histories of 12th graders will vary greatly from those written by 3rd graders, but all students can come to their own conclusions and support those conclusions with evidence from the data they collected through the community investigation process.

Conclusion

Planning and conducting a community history inquiry project is an exciting adventure for students of all ages. In the process, they will learn valuable firsthand research skills, acquire stronger connections to people and organizations in the local community, and develop a greater appreciation for the community and its history.

CHAPTER FIVE

Exploring Our Nation's History

Rahima C. Wade

An in-depth understanding of the local community's history needs to be situated within an understanding of national conditions and events related to the issue under study. This chapter describes methods and resources for learning about social and environmental issues in U.S. history.

Begin with Questions

Thus far in their project, your students have developed an in-depth understanding of the local history of their selected issue and have written a community history, relying on various sources of information to support their conclusions. Next, ask students to brainstorm questions they have about the history of the issue in the national context. If deemed relevant, you may want to confine the study of national history to a specific time period or event. For example, if the issue under study is poverty, you might want to have students learn about the Great Depression, or if child labor is the topic, you might want to focus students' inquiries on the labor movement in the early 1900s. However, one should be careful not to give the impression that these issues were a problem only during the selected time period. Most social and environmental issues have a long legacy in our nation's history, and are still being addressed today.

Students should be encouraged to brainstorm a wide variety of questions about their topic. If desired, this list can then be narrowed down before beginning to research. Here is a set of questions that might be applied to the study of any issue in a national context:

- When did this problem emerge in our nation's history?
- How does the evolution of the problem parallel or differ from what was happening in our community?
- How did ordinary citizens and grassroots groups deal with this problem?
- How did our nation's leaders deal with this problem? Did they pass legislation to try to resolve it in some way? What other measures did they take to try to lessen or eliminate the problem?
- Is the problem still present throughout U.S. society today?

If not, why not? What happened that led to the elimination of this problem in some locations? If yes, what are people trying to do to change the situation? What strategies appear to be promising?

After students have agreed upon a set of questions to guide their research, they can begin to learn about the issue nationally.

Beyond the Textbook

While your social studies textbook may have one or a few sections that are relevant to understanding the history of your selected issue nationally, it is likely that you and your students will need to go beyond the textbook and seek out other resources that can provide multiple perspectives and a more in-depth understanding of the issue. Possible resources include books, websites, and primary sources.

Books

If possible, obtain a variety of books about the issue, including those written for the grade level you are teaching, as well as more advanced resources and/or books for younger students. Have students read different books or parts of them, and then compare what they learned. Encourage students to think of themselves as history detectives, attempting to solve the "mystery" of the events of the past. What facts are supported by most or all of the books? What different interpretations of some events are presented? Why do you think that historians differ about these events? What do you think is the most compelling evidence or argument for a certain interpretation?

Websites

The World Wide Web is a great source of information on almost any subject. Simply putting the title of the issue your class is studying in one of many search engines is likely to point to hundreds, if not thousands, of websites. One of the challenges of web searches is not to get lost in the voluminous amount of information on a topic. For this reason, teachers may want to pre-select websites for the class to use in their research. Another challenge is to find reliable and credible information. Make sure to have your students refine their searches as much as possible and look carefully at the source of the information.

Primary Sources

If possible, locate materials that were produced during the time period under study. Primary sources will allow your students to think like historians, as they uncover information from a variety of perspectives and attempt to draw conclusions about the past. For example, students might examine government documents, newspaper articles, or public notices related to their issue. Here is a list of just a few of the types of primary sources that might prove useful in a project modeled on those of CiviConnections: letters, government documents, newspaper articles, maps, posters, diaries, medical records, court records, testimonies, and photos.

Many primary sources can be found in historical societies, museums, and public libraries. For topical packets of primary sources assembled for classroom use, contact Jackdaw publications (1-800-962-9101, www.jackdaw.com). Another source for primary sources, as well as timelines, lists, and charts on various issues and events in American history, is the *American History Teacher's Book of Lists* by Fay R. Hansen (from The Center for Applied Research in Education in West Nyack, New York and listed on Amazon.com).

Constructing a Narrative

When students have completed their research on our nation's history concerning the issue they are studying, they should construct a narrative that compares and contrasts their local community's history with national history. There are many possibilities for how students could present their learning. Consider the following options, based on students' interests and abilities: an essay, a PowerPoint presentation, two parallel timelines, a poster, or a conceptual map or web. Students could work on any of these projects individually, with a partner, or in a team. In an elementary classroom, you may want to guide students' comparisons and narrative construction in a whole-class discussion.

Conclusion

Comparing local history and national history relevant to a selected social or environmental issue will aid students' understanding of the connections between their community and national events. They will also encounter additional ideas for strategic change that may be applied to their efforts to "make history" by serving their local community. 🐚

CHAPTER SIX

Examining Government Documents

RAHIMA C. WADE

This chapter explains how you and your students can use government documents, such as the Bill of Rights, the Constitution, or the Universal Declaration of Human Rights, to reflect on how students might change or improve their community. These documents and others listed here highlight essential principles of democratic living and social justice.

The Declaration of Independence, the United States Constitution, and the Bill of Rights

These three documents were foundational in setting up the new government of the United States of America. Students can examine these papers to develop an understanding of the basic democratic principles adhered to by statesmen and government leaders of the time. While limited to white males, the documents did set forth a set of rights and responsibilities of democratic citizens. Later amendments asserted that people of color and women should also benefit from the rights and responsibilities accorded to all U.S. citizens.

Students can examine these documents (or simplified, abbreviated versions) as they reflect on the rights and responsibilities related to the issue they are studying in their local community. For example, if the class is investigating voting rights as their selected community issue, these documents as well as the 15th and 19th Amendments to the Constitution will be informative. For details on the history of all of these documents, as well as the full text, go to ourdocuments.gov.

The United Nations Universal Declaration of Human Rights

Adopted by the General Assembly of the United Nations on December 10, 1948, the Universal Declaration of Human Rights (UDHR) proclaims a broad spectrum of economic, social, cultural, political, and civil rights for all of the world's people. Article 2 of the UDHR reads, "Everyone is entitled to all the rights and freedoms set forth in this Declaration, without distinction of any kind, such as race, color, sex, language, religion, political or other opinion, national or social origin, property, birth, or other

status." It is easy to see how just this article alone is relevant for the following community issues: hunger, homelessness, violence, hate crime, and racial profiling. Following is a brief description of the 30 articles in the UDHR. For a complete transcript, click on the featured link at www.hrusa.org.

ARTICLE 1 – Right to Equality
ARTICLE 2 – Freedom from Discrimination
ARTICLE 3 – Right to Life, Liberty, and Personal Security
ARTICLE 4 – Freedom from Slavery
ARTICLE 5 – Freedom from Torture and Degrading Treatment
ARTICLE 6 – Right to Recognition as a Person before the Law
ARTICLE 7 – Right to Equality before the Law
ARTICLE 8 – Right to Remedy by Competent Tribunal
ARTICLE 9 – Freedom from Arbitrary Arrest and Exile
ARTICLE 10 – Right to Fair Public Hearing
ARTICLE 11 – Right to be Considered Innocent until Proven Guilty
ARTICLE 12 – Freedom from Interference with Privacy, Family, Home, and Correspondence
ARTICLE 13 – Right to Free Movement in and out of the Country
ARTICLE 14 – Right to Asylum in Other Countries from Persecution
ARTICLE 15 – Right to a Nationality and the Freedom to Change Nationality
ARTICLE 16 – Right to Marriage and Family
ARTICLE 17 – Right to Own Property
ARTICLE 18 – Freedom of Belief and Religion
ARTICLE 19 – Freedom of Opinion and Information
ARTICLE 20 – Right of Peaceful Assembly and Association
ARTICLE 21 – Right to Participate in Government and in Free Elections
ARTICLE 22 – Right to Social Security

ARTICLE 23 – Right to Desirable Work and to Join
Trade Unions

ARTICLE 24 – Right to Rest and Leisure

ARTICLE 25 – Right to Adequate Living Standard

ARTICLE 26 – Right to Education

ARTICLE 27 – Right to Participate in the Cultural Life of
the Community

ARTICLE 28 – Right to a Social Order that Articulates
this Document

ARTICLE 29 – Community Duties Essential to Free and
Full Development

ARTICLE 30 – Freedom from State or Personal Interference
in the Above Rights

If your students have selected a community issue specific to children, you should consider using the United Nations Declaration of the Rights of the Child, adopted by the UN General Assembly on November 20, 1959. For a full text of the document, go to www.un.org/cyberschoolbus/humanrights/resources/child.asp. Following is an abbreviated and simplified version, especially useful for elementary-age students.

1. All children have the same rights, whether they are rich or poor, boy or girl, black, brown, white, or yellow skinned.
2. All children should have the chance to grow up healthy and safe, and in a good place to live.
3. All children have the right to a name and a country of their own.
4. All children have the right to nourishing food, a decent home, proper clothing, a safe place to play, and good medical care.
5. Children who are blind, deaf, crippled, sick, or have a learning disability should be given special care and attention.
6. All children need to grow up in an environment of love and care.
7. All children should have good schools to go to which help them learn and play.
8. When a child is in danger, he or she should be quickly cared for.
9. Children should not be treated harshly or cruelly, or made to work outside the home before they are old enough.
10. Children have the right to be brought up in the spirit of understanding, tolerance, friendship, and peace.

Milestone Documents

As your students learn about their selected issue in both local and national history, they will also benefit from examining government documents to see how this issue is supported in our basic democratic principles. The 100 Milestone Documents feature thousands of public laws, Supreme Court decisions, speeches, treaties, amendments, and other documents that have shaped the course of U.S. history from 1776 to 1965. The documents include the Declaration of Independence, the Louisiana Purchase Treaty, the Patent for the Cotton Gin, the Sherman Anti-Trust Act, and 96 others. The creators of the list decided to include documents only up to 1965, because, according to the National Center for History in the Schools, "Historians can never attain complete objectivity, but they tend to fall shortest of the goal when they deal with current or very recent events." To read any of the 100 Milestone Documents, go to ourdocuments.gov.

Connecting Milestone Documents with Local History

There are many possible ways to integrate the study of some of the Milestone Documents with local historical inquiry. For example, classes studying the issue of racism in the local community might want to examine one or more of the following: the Chinese Exclusion Act (1882), *Plessy v. Ferguson* (1896), *Brown v. Board of Education* (1954), and the Civil Rights Act (1964), to name just a few of the possibilities. The Act Establishing Yellowstone National Park (1872) might be interesting reading for students working on public land use issues. On the topic of child labor, the Keating-Owen Child Labor Act (1916) might be most suitable. Elementary and middle school students could read or listen to summaries of these documents, whereas high school students could read them in their entirety.

Government Documents Resource List

In addition to the websites mentioned above, check out the following for government documents and resources for teaching with government documents.

memory.loc.gov/ammem/ndlpedu/lessons/98/local/intro.html

The collection of primary source materials constitutes the principal activity of a year-long American Studies class focusing on historiography and the use of primary sources. Students collect primary source materials from their families or local communities. In analyzing these primary sources, students examine the interplay between national, state, local, and personal history. Over a period of several weeks, students produce a digital collection modeled on the Library of Congress' American Memory.

ourdocuments.gov
This is the U.S. federal government's website that includes the 100 Milestone Documents.

gateway.library.uiuc.edu/doc
This is a U.S. Government Documents Library housed at the University of Illinois Urbana-Champaign.

memory.loc.gov/ammem/amhome.html
American Memory is a gateway to government documents and many more primary source materials relating to the history and culture of the United States. The site offers more than 7 million digital items from more than 100 historical collections.

www.archives.gov/digital_classroom/index.html
The U.S. National Archives and Records Administration (NARA) Teaching with Documents website groups key documents by time period in U.S. history.

www.lib.umich.edu/govdocs/fedhis.html#frus
The University of Michigan Documents Center offers a comprehensive list of websites for accessing Federal Government resources and historic documents.

www.edteck.com/dbq
The Teaching with Documents website, maintained by Peter Pappas, gathers an exceptional collection of student worksheets and guidelines for analyzing government documents and other types of primary sources.

civnet.org/resources/resources_frameset.htm
Civnet's Teacher and Student Resources feature a collection of some of the world's great historic documents and speeches pertaining to civics, democracy, human rights, tolerance, and freedom (e.g., the Magna Carta, U.S. Declaration of Independence, and Universal Declaration of Human Rights).

bensguide.gpo.gov
Ben's Guide to the U.S. Government, a service of the U.S. Government Printing Office, is an excellent resource for all grades. There are age-appropriate elementary, middle school, and high school links for learning about government documents and the history of the U.S. government.

Conclusion
Government documents are an important primary source that students can use to further understand local and national history. In addition, students benefit from learning about how citizens in a democracy work for social change and assure individual rights and communal responsibilities through legal means such as laws, treaties, and court cases. Finally, many of our government documents affirm our highest ideals for living together peacefully and equitably. Students can gain both inspiration and ideas for further social change efforts as they explore this important component of our history.

CHAPTER SEVEN

Improving Our Community

Rahima C. Wade

Having reflected on the principles in government documents, as well as having studied the evolution of the selected issue in both their local community and the nation, students are now positioned to plan and implement ways they can take action to improve their community. This chapter covers options for indirect and direct service activities, as well as advocacy strategies, students can employ to create positive change.

Brainstorm Opportunities for Change
Ask students to consider how they might take action to improve the problem or issue they have been studying. They should think about ways they can get involved in local change, as well as ideas for how they can influence public policy on a state or national level. Before brainstorming, students should review what they have learned about citizens' efforts to make a difference in regard to their selected issue. Which actions have been most influential? Which ideas have not been tried but might prove useful? Encourage students to think about the following types of action as they brainstorm ideas:

- Direct service — working directly in the community with people, animals, or in natural environments. Examples: building a nature trail, bagging groceries at the Crisis Center, reading to homebound senior citizens, or preparing and serving a meal at the local soup kitchen.
- Indirect service — fundraisers or collections of various materials. Examples: recycling in the school, canned food drive, clothing drive, bake sale, movie-and-popcorn fundraiser, read-a-thon, or adopt-a-(whale, manatee, rainforest area) activities.
- Advocacy — letter writing, petitions, or campaigns to influence people's views on an issue. Examples: letters to the editor, proposal to the local city council, petition for a new local policy or law, or writing to government officials.

In the truest spirit of brainstorming, do not dismiss or criticize any of the students' ideas at this point. Instead, the focus should be on generating as many ideas as possible for how students might create positive change in regard to their issue. Record the students' ideas on large chart paper for future use. Also, feel free to contribute your own ideas to the brainstormed list as well.

Introduce Decision-Making Criteria
After you and your students have created a comprehensive list of possible ways to make a difference, it is important to introduce the criteria to guide the decision-making process. Consider which of the following criteria are relevant for your project:

- Time — How much class time can be devoted to service activities? How much out-of-school time can be required or are students willing to contribute?
- Funds — What funds have been budgeted for the service activities? If additional funds are needed, what organizations or individuals might support these actions?
- Interest — Which of the ideas brainstormed are most interesting to students? Which one(s) do they want to implement?
- Impact — Which of the possible activities is likely to have the most impact on the community or on the issue nationally?
- Capability — Which ideas will students be able to carry out? If adult assistance or supervision is required, are parents, community members, or other school staff available to participate?

Choosing One or More Service Projects
Decide in advance if the class will complete one or more service activities all together, or if pairs, committees, or small groups of students can work together on different actions. You and your students can informally discuss their brainstormed ideas in light of the criteria presented, or complete a more structured process to choose one or more service activities.

Figure 1. Decision-Making Grid Chart — Ideas on Homelessness

Idea	Time	Funds	Interest	Impact	Capability
Bake sale to raise funds	1	1	1	2	1
Open a new shelter	3	3	1	1	3
Serve a weekly meal at the shelter	2	2	2	2	1
Advocacy to city councilors	1	1	2	2	1
Get jobs for homeless people	3	1	3	1	3
Start a mail service at the soup kitchen	2	1	1	2	2
Get churches to provide overflow housing for the shelter	2	2	3	1	2
Write to U.S. President	1	1	3	3	1

As an example of the latter, a grid chart could be created and filled in similar to the one in Figure 1.

In this chart, 1 = easily meets this criteria, 2 = minimally meets this criteria, and 3 = does not meet this criteria. In this example, the best choices have the lowest scores. Thus, the students in this 10th grade class decided to have a bake sale to raise funds for the local homeless shelter, write letters to the local city council advocating for a new shelter, and start a mail service at the local soup kitchen for individuals who are homeless. These ideas incorporate the three types of service: indirect service, advocacy, and direct service, respectively. The teacher and class agreed that everyone would write letters, but that the class would work in two groups on the bake sale and the mail service.

The grid chart strategy will allow the most practical and doable ideas to surface. But what if your students have a grand idea about which they are truly excited? If you are willing to support your students in completing a large project, by all means, do so.

Planning for Success

Spending time in the planning phase can help to create successful service experiences for students and the community. You may want to revisit the essential elements of high-quality service-learning discussed in Chapter 2. Also, think about the following questions in planning for success:

- How will you prepare community agency members for working with students?
- How will you prepare students for their service-learning activities?
- How much planning time do those coordinating the project need to develop an effective program?
- Have you planned for community and student input, training, orientations, supplies, transportation, the service activities, academic integration, structured reflection, publicity, and evaluation?
- Who is responsible for coordinating the service activities onsite?
- Who is responsible for getting supplies, coordinating transportation, and planning activities?
- How will you monitor the actual service activities?
- How are the service activities being integrated with the academic curriculum?
- How will you give participants opportunities to reflect on their service activities?
- Who has the time and expertise to be the problem solver or troubleshooter?
- How can participants get the help they need in their service activities?
- In what ways will you have students reflect on what they are learning in your project?
- How will the participants in your project be recognized for their efforts?
- How will you evaluate the effectiveness of your project?
- How can you engender broad-based support for your

project?
- In what ways can you publicize the successes of your project?
- How can you collect feedback from a variety of sources to improve your project?

Conclusion
Careful planning and consideration of alternatives for improving the community will increase the likelihood of students making meaningful contributions. Students should begin with an evaluation of the best options for creating positive change, based on what they have learned from the local and national historical studies. They can then use the various brainstorming, questioning, and decision-making strategies outlined in this chapter to choose the best options for serving the community through indirect, direct, or advocacy efforts. 🖎

CHAPTER EIGHT

Celebrating Service and Learning

RAHIMA C. WADE

Each project modeled on CiviConnections results in a community-wide celebration of students' learning and service. This chapter addresses options for when and where to hold the celebration, who to invite, and how to feature students' accomplishments in ways that will engender inspiration and further action on the part of the community members who attend the celebration.

Celebrating Students' Efforts

A community-wide celebration serves several purposes as a culminating event for your project. First, the event gives everyone a chance to celebrate the students' hard work, both in their community investigations and in their service to the community. Second, students' preparation for the public display and/or presentations gives them an opportunity to reflect on their efforts and to discern what are the most important aspects of their work to share with others. Finally, the celebration will teach others about the community issue your students chose, and hopefully inspire them to take action on this issue, both locally and nationally.

Who to Invite and Where to Celebrate: Defining "Community"

You and your students need to decide how large an event to hold and whom you want to invite. This might depend in part on the particular project, who was involved, and how large an event the class envisions. Thus, the celebration could be held for any of the following communities:

- School community – This event would be attended by teachers, students, staff, principal, and parents. The celebration could be held at the school in the evening or on a weekend.
- Local community or neighborhood community – The celebration would be attended by the school community, as well as local neighbors and community residents. The event could be held at the school or at a local community center, public library meeting room, or other location in the neighborhood.
- City-wide event – This celebration would be open to the general public, as well as invited guests from the community and others listed previously. The celebration could still be held at the school or in any public meeting place in the town or city.

As you consider where to hold the community celebration, consider also which locations are more likely to draw the people you hope will attend. While the school may seem like the easiest place, a community location might be better in terms of attracting residents of your city or town. How many people do you anticipate will attend? Make sure the space you have reserved will hold the projected number of attendees. If a very large number of people will attend, check the acoustics of the room and get a microphone, if needed, so student speakers will be heard clearly.

Is it possible to station a display in a public location for a few weeks? If so, this would provide additional opportunities for others to learn and be inspired by the students' work. Do some public sites (such as a post office, shopping mall, or library) draw considerable traffic on their own? If possible, involve students in the decisions associated with where, when, and how to organize the celebration and public display. Student ownership in planning will contribute to students' comfort and excitement about these important culminating events.

Options for Celebrating Learning and Service

After deciding when and where to hold the celebration, and whom you hope will attend, there are still many decisions to be made. How will the learning and service be featured? Here are some possible activities you and your students might want to consider:

- Student awards – Presented by the principal, the mayor, or the director of a community organization involved in the project.
- Display – Photos with captions, students' written work,

or other project "artifacts" can be mounted on posters, a wall, or bulletin boards.

- Multi-media presentation – A video on the project, or a slide show set to music or student narration, could be shown.
- Refreshments – Perhaps a few parents would organize something or you could provide light snacks.
- Student speeches – Students who wish to could each speak briefly about a selected aspect of their work.
- Community speakers – Invite those who were involved with or touched by the project to share their perspectives, or invite the mayor or principal to make a speech in recognition of the students' efforts.
- Service activities – You could set up an optional donation bowl to contribute funds toward addressing your issue, or have postcards and stamps available for attendees to engage in an advocacy activity.
- Handouts – Consider having students create a handout for celebration attendees that provides a brief description of what they learned and how they made a difference, as well as ideas for further action and needed contact information, so that more people can get involved with the issue.

These are just a few of the many options possible for an informative and fun celebration. Be creative, invite student input, and welcome assistance from parents or other community members who would like to be involved in planning and facilitating this event.

Publicizing the Celebration

Don't wait until the last minute to set the date for and publicize the celebration. Give everyone plenty of advance notice about when and where the event will be held. Students can make personal invitations for parents and selected community members. You could also publicize the event in the local newspaper, community organization newsletters, the school newsletter, local radio and TV, and other outlets in your community. All of these publication outlets take some lead time, sometimes a few weeks or more, so begin planning your celebration at least a month in advance.

Other Questions to Think About...

- How long do we want the celebration to last?
- Will parents or students bring refreshments?
- Will there be set up? Clean up?
- Are there costs associated with reserving a selected public space?
- How much time do we want to devote to planning the celebration?
- Do we need other adults to help supervise the celebration?
- Will students be involved in making presentations or giving "tours" of the displays?

Conclusion

The community celebration serves several purposes. It gives students an opportunity to reflect on their learning and experience, and to consider how to present their learning to others. The celebration also provides a suitable means for assessing students' learning from their experiences. Finally, the celebration serves to inspire local community members to get involved with this issue and to recognize the students' efforts.

Part Three
Projects in Action

CHAPTER NINE

Food for the Poor

Poverty and hunger are visible and persistent problems in many communities across the United States. Not surprisingly, these issues were frequently at the center of CiviConnections projects. In this chapter, we look at how students, teachers, and community members in Colorado, California, and Oregon initiated and shaped projects focused on learning about the history of local poverty and helping those in need.

Each of these projects follows the same six steps in the process: choosing an issue and guiding question, investigating our community's history, exploring our nation's history, examining government documents, improving our community, and celebrating service and learning. There are additional similar elements among these projects—all three involve middle-school-age students working with food pantries—yet there are important differences as well. As you read the stories here, consider how students' interests, community needs, available resources, and teachers' curricular requirements uniquely shape each project.

The Hidden Faces of Hunger

Lincoln Junior High, Fort Collins, Colorado

Megan Baker

Lincoln Junior High International Baccalaureate World School in Fort Collins, Colorado has a 50/50 Latino/White student body, with 60 percent qualified for Free and Reduced Lunch. Despite the joys and challenges of diversity that Lincoln faces, we are a service-focused school. Students and staff collect dozens of boxes of food for the local food bank every fall, quilt and crochet hundreds of blankets for the county Humane Society, and organize annual drives for shoes and toiletries. We are also the first school in our district to sponsor a Habitat for Humanity house, an effort that required us to raise $50,000 in cash and in-kind donations this year. These and many other projects help us instill in our students a sense that, no matter what their circumstances, they can still serve.

Through our CiviConnections project, we wanted to connect our diverse student populations with each other, and help our students make meaningful, real-world connections to our 7th-9th grade geography and history curricula. It soon became clear that hunger would be our focus. All of us had been actively involved in Lincoln's ongoing participation in "Cans Around the Oval," an annual food drive put on by Colorado State University students on their campus common, known as "The Oval." What better way to expand our involvement than to really dig into the causes of hunger around the world and in our own community?

Thus, the Hidden Faces of Hunger project was born.

The students in my classes began their investigation into hunger with a look at the fundamentals of the issue. I asked my students to reflect upon and write about a time when they'd been truly hungry. The responses were varied, and reflected their general lack of experience. Though a few could describe the pangs of wondering where their next meal would come from, most had only missed a meal or two, and experienced nothing but a growling stomach. A small-group, definition-building activity gave us a chance to discuss and understand terms like malnourishment, chronic hunger, and famine. A guided internet investigation helped the students understand categories and statistics surrounding worldwide hunger issues, with each student using a UN website and other sites to discover causes of child mortality around the world, regions with the most people living with hunger, and the impacts of malnutrition over the life-cycle.

As a result of discussions following these activities, the essential questions of our unit became, "What happens to a community when the needs of all its members are not met? How should that community respond?" Hunger, my students had discovered, is more than an economic issue. "How can hunger be political?" my mostly-privileged students asked me. Hurricane Katrina provided timely and poignant fodder for discussion, as our project began with the start of school in late August. As students watched newscasts describing the desperate looting of Wal-Marts and other stores in the New Orleans area, and the compassionate clerks, managers, and police officers who turned a blind eye to theft in the face of tragedy and need, class discussions got personal. "But why can't we guarantee these things to all citizens?" some of my students asked. Others expressed the opinion that the government should not be responsible for providing food.

Their investigations into the U.S. Bill of Rights and the UN Universal Declaration of Human Rights (UDHR) provided some answers. U.S. citizens are not protected from hunger, they learned, and all the nations of the world have not adopted, nor can they carry out, the provisions mentioned in Article 25 of the UN UDHR: "Everyone has the right to a standard of living adequate for the health and well-being of himself and of his family, including food, clothing, housing and medical care and necessary social services, and the right to security in the event of unemployment, sickness, disability, widowhood, old age or other lack of livelihood in circumstances beyond his control."

Final essay reflections on the question of governmental responsibility for issues of hunger centered around tragedy and national emergency. Most students argued that—at least during times of personal, regional, or national emergency—citizens should be provided with emergency provisions for food, clothing, and shelter. How this could be done was not clear, but student speculation on the necessary systems and institutions proved to be an interesting segue to the next phase of our CiviConnections project—developing a service activity.

When Jill, the local Food Bank Volunteer Coordinator, came to speak to our classes, the students were ready with questions. Jill painted for them a picture of the typical food bank client—hardworking, of no particular ethnicity, and of almost any age. In other words, my students learned, there is no typical food recipient at the Larimer County Food Bank. Almost anyone can be hungry or become hungry due to lay-off, health issues, or simply lack of adequate pay. Jill helped students understand that sometimes their neighbors have to make difficult monetary choices, paying bills rather than buying food, or going hungry in order to feed their children.

What, my students asked, does the Larimer County Food Bank need right now? Jill identified major ongoing needs: donated food and publicity. The annual Cans Around the Oval food drive was coming up in October, and the food bank needed Lincoln to participate again in the big way we always had. In addition, the food bank had opened up a new program, the Kids' Café, in June. Kids' Café provides free dinner meals to needy students during the school year, and breakfast and lunch during the summer. The idea is to provide the meals that aren't available at school through the Free and Reduced meals

programs. Kids' Café is housed at the Boys' & Girls' Club next door to our school, but many Lincoln students and staff didn't even know it existed. As a result of Jill's presentation, my students and I were inspired to create a Lincoln Junior High IB World School PR campaign for the Larimer County Food Bank.

Zana's ESL students, on the other hand, chose to do most of the legwork around our Cans Around the Oval effort. They would research and create educational materials around community hunger for a display case outside Zana's classroom. In addition, they would organize the nitty-gritty details of the food drive—collecting the donations from mentoring classes, and boxing and stacking the donated food for pick-up. Finally, if Zana and I could figure out how to make it work, they would collaborate with my students to translate the food bank public relations materials my students were developing into Spanish.

Through the end of September, our classes worked on their service assignments. Zana's students researched hunger issues, finding compelling photos and simple statistics to create their display, focused on catching the attention of Lincoln's diverse student population. My students researched their various assignments, and planned and executed their PR offerings. They made commercials, flyers, and posters advertising Cans Around the Oval. We had signed an official competition pledge against the Colorado State University Student Council, known as ASCSU, and our success was extremely important. We had to win the free dance on the college campus they'd promised us, or we'd owe them a giant pizza party—and pizza and soda for 50 college kids would cost our school dearly. As word of our students' educational efforts spread, a technology teacher even asked our permission to get in on the service project—could her students design food drive flyers as a class project? Suddenly, we had 30 more project participants than we had counted on! Motivated by the sports-related humor of the food drive commercials and the kid prose of their peers' PR brochures and signs, mentoring classes around the building began to collect food in earnest by the end of September. The annual competition would close on October 14th, with our donations to be collected and boxed for weighing on October 13th.

Other students created PR materials for Kids' Café. "What do you do if you can't feed your family?" a trifold brochure asked parents. "TEACHERS! Do You Know a Hungry Kid? Well, Feed Them!" a flyer for teachers proclaimed. A student poster featured the following words on top of a rainbow, "Are You Hungry? Do You Need a Free Meal?" Students posted their informational art everywhere they could think to put it around the school—on our courtyard windows and brick walls, in the locker bays, on the Student Services lobby table, and even in the bathroom stalls.

On October 13th, a core group of students gathered in our auditorium. Using hand signals, I explained their job: roll dollies to each classroom, stack boxes of food, and bring them back to the auditorium for re-packaging. Food had to be sorted by type and packed according to strict food bank rules, and it had to be done fast. Students spread out across the school and rolled boxes up and down the halls. Within one class period, the auditorium stairs were filled with bursting boxes and we had a huge mess. Within two more class periods, we'd sorted, re-boxed, and stacked it all. Final total = 101 boxes of food. Trucks rolled up to our front door the next day and took our donated food to the CSU campus for the official weigh-in—which registered 4,362 pounds, all from the students and staff of the most poverty-impacted junior high in the Poudre School District.

We celebrated our service to the Larimer County Food Bank in two ways. On October 14th, we took 100 students to CSU's Oval for the official Cans Around the Oval event. When they arrived, they were ushered onto a make-shift stage to be photographed with event dignitaries. Next, they started their real job—to surround the CSU Oval, approximately one quarter mile in circumference, with a symbolic ring of cans. Students ran back and forth for an hour, bringing cans to peers who placed them on the curb next to each other. After an hour and 15 minutes, the curb surrounding the Oval was totally covered with cans, and the campus paper and Denver news channels had interviewed and photographed our students for their evening editions. Though other junior highs had contributed more pounds, none could say what we could claim. Seventy five percent of the students who accompanied us to the Oval to stack cans that day received a sack lunch at school expense because they qualify for Free and Reduced Lunch. Yet, there they were, toting huge boxes of donated food to create a quarter-mile-long symbol aimed at ending community hunger.

A follow-up assembly became another celebration. Winning classes at each grade level received prizes for their food drive contributions, and all students who worked on the Hidden Faces of Hunger project were recognized for their participation. Special recognition was given to those students who went out of their way to collect food in their neighborhoods, and we shared hunger statistics and food bank information with the whole school community. It seemed that we'd accomplished the goal of raising school awareness of hunger issues and food bank services.

Though our project was very successful, there are always aspects of teaching that can be improved. One of our original goals was to use the project to create connections between our diverse populations. By and large, that didn't happen. The act of translating all materials proved too cumbersome and time-consuming, and that natural way of partnering our students together collapsed. PR materials went out independently in Spanish and English, but not in dual-language format. During the Cans Around the Oval can-stacking project on October 14th, our kids were segregated by translation needs into separate buses and groups. Even when they arrived on campus and got down to the business of moving and stacking food, they self-selected into language groups. Every chance we had, we teamed students from diverse backgrounds. Only when we gave them a push, did they begin to mingle. If we had to do it all over again, we'd force the issue of connection over the course of the whole Hidden Faces of Hunger project more than we did. We learned that we need to push back against the time and structural constraints in our school that support students' natural tendencies to divide into ethnic groups. Service is a great place to break down barriers, because all kinds of students can find ways to be successful, and all students' contributions can be celebrated.

Six months later, Kids' Café posters still hang in the bathroom stalls at Lincoln Junior High. Full-color Larimer County Food Bank services flyers, created by my students and aimed at my colleagues, decorate the door of the staff lounge. One in seven Larimer County residents will access the food bank this year. If our efforts help even one student get a meal he or she needs, I know we've succeeded.

In addition to the author, Zana Kamberi and Nicole Seidow were team teachers on this CiviConnections project.

❧

From Apathy to Advocacy
Prairie Middle School, Woodburn, Oregon

MARK LIDTKE

The students of French Prairie Middle School vividly know and understand the culture of poverty. Although there are some students from affluent and middle-class families, a vast majority come from families that struggle just to make ends meet. So when we began initial discussions with our social studies classes to select a community issue for this project, we had a good idea of what the students might be thinking.

Our initial class sessions involved having each student brainstorm individually, and then collectively in small groups, our basic human rights and survival needs. We then categorized and discussed their responses. Next, the students began focusing on the specific needs of their community—Woodburn, Oregon. As suspected, the students overwhelmingly focused on two basic needs: food and shelter. After more class discussion, we reached consensus and the students selected "Quality of Life: Helping Those in Need" as their final issue to investigate.

From a teaching standpoint, investigating the issue in Woodburn's history was the most difficult aspect of this project. There simply was little, if any, curriculum material in the student textbooks that could be used to study our issue as it applied to the Woodburn area. In addition, Woodburn is a relatively small community—other than a few minor primary documents, there wasn't much information available. So while we kept the focus on Woodburn as much as possible, we expanded our search to include information relating to the Willamette Valley. The Oregon Historical Society, the Oregon State University Extension Family and Development office, the Oregon Food Bank, and Oregon Public Broadcasting all proved to be extremely valuable sources of information. In addition, we used various newspaper articles and several old books dealing with Oregon history. It took long hours to put the pieces of the puzzle together that would allow students to construct a solid understanding of how people have helped those in need throughout Woodburn's history.

After assembling our resources, students formed cooperative learning groups and began their work as history detectives. The students began with two guiding questions. The first was "How large was the housing and food status problem?" The second question was "How did people help those in need?" Students examined documents dating from the early nineteenth century to the present. They worked at describing and charting their findings, and then reporting back to the rest of the class.

We then focused on Oregon's current status as one of the states with the largest hunger problem in the country. This part of the study especially fascinated and puzzled the students. At first they found it difficult to believe that a state like Oregon with such a strong agricultural base could lead the nation in hunger. As they dug into the issue though, they realized that there were economic factors at work that forced people to choose between buying food and paying for other basic necessities. They developed a great deal of empathy for those in need.

After we finished examining the local history of our issue, we shifted our studies to explore hunger in our national history.

Unlike our challenging search for information about Woodburn and the Willamette Valley, there was a wealth of material conveniently available at the school library, in student textbooks, and on the Internet. Working individually and in small groups, students conducted research beginning with the first European settlements to contemporary times, and reported their findings to the class. Our next step was to inspect government documents. We looked at the United States Constitution and the Bill of Rights, and we also reviewed the State of Oregon Constitution and Bill of Rights.

In analyzing historical quotes, students found that many inauguration speeches strongly promoted community service and frequently dealt with the issues of hunger and poverty. We found pertinent and inspiring quotes by civic leaders such as Martin Luther King, Jr. and César Chavez, whose thoughts proved to be especially inspiring to our Hispanic students.

Early in the project, we talked with different community leaders, who suggested we meet with Nancy Stone, director of the local food bank. Located in downtown Woodburn, the food bank has filled a critical and growing need for the community. In 1999, 500 individuals a month benefited from its services. Six years later, during the month when French Prairie students began their work there, the food bank fed 3,400 individuals, including 1,671 children.

Nancy was remarkably helpful and enthusiastic. After a discussion of what we hoped to accomplish and a presentation of our timeline, she immediately handed over a key to the building, gave her phone numbers, and pledged her support. She was extremely patient in answering all of our questions. She also enjoyed stopping by the food bank to meet with the students, encourage them, and offer an occasional treat. Nancy was a strong role model, in particular for our large base of Hispanic students. Her partnership and support demonstrated the value and potential of collaborating with community members to promote service learning.

For three days a week after school, students stacked and arranged shelves, sacked food, cleaned shelves, recycled cardboard, swept floors, and helped alphabetize files. Students also helped the food bank through in-class activities. Working with the student council, the students sponsored a school canned food drive that netted over 1,600 pounds of food. This involved students advertising the event, collecting and sorting the food at school, and then stocking it at the food bank. We also incorporated a letter-writing unit that resulted in over $4,000 dollars in donations, and a successful Saturday rummage sale that generated badly needed funds for the holiday season.

Students also composed letters as an advocacy tool to reduce hunger both nationally and internationally. Using somber facts and statistics that they learned in class, students wrote to the Oregon Congressional delegation and to many United States Senators, urging action to reduce hunger locally, throughout the United States, and worldwide. Many of the students received personal replies and realized the impact that they can make as advocates for change.

At the beginning of the project, we invited the local director of Habitat for Humanity to make presentations to our classes. The presentation was excellent and the organization was eager to involve our students. However, the time constraints of the project worked against us; there were simply no building projects in the Woodburn area available. However, we were able to place several eighth grade students in leadership positions with that organization. These students will lead efforts at Woodburn High School throughout their time there, to involve the student body as that organization moves forward with housing projects in Woodburn.

The community celebration was a huge success and a definite highlight of our CiviConnections experience. The students wrote personal letters of invitation to parents, donors, school board members, Woodburn School District administrative staff, Woodburn City Council members, and other civic dignitaries. Requests to local merchants for refreshment donations resulted in an abundance of food and beverages. Students also designed and created decorations and displays, and spent several hectic hours after school decorating the cafeteria and arranging the refreshments.

The celebration event was well attended. In addition to the students and their families, most of the invited guests also came. Along with Principal Betty Komp and food bank director Nancy Stone, we made brief remarks about the impact of the CiviConnections program on Woodburn and the students. We then introduced the students, who came forward and received recognition awards. Students who completed in-class advocacy work received citizenship certificates, and students who worked after school at the food bank received medals. Many of the students were so thrilled with their medals that they wore them the next day to school.

Based on the success of our initial efforts, we are continuing to involve students in hunger relief efforts. As part of French Prairie's after-school enrichment program, every student at school has the opportunity to volunteer at the food bank one day a week for 1.5 hours. While the program was originally implemented only for seventh and eighth graders, we are now including sixth graders, who have been enthusiastic participants in the continuing program. Even though students in the after-school program have a wide range of fun and exciting options to choose from, including swimming, cooking, various art and technology classes, as well as martial arts, the food bank option, officially titled "Be a Food Bank Super Hero," has consistently been among the most popular activities.

However, the continuation of our partnership with the food bank is uncertain. Director Nancy Stone's husband received a career promotion, and her family has moved away. The new leadership team is not as enthusiastic about working with middle school students as Stone was, and has limited the work that students can do to stocking and cleaning. We believe that unless the students are welcomed, appreciated, and allowed to perform meaningful tasks, this community-service option needs to be carefully re-evaluated.

All in all, our program was and continues to be successful. CiviConnections unified the students and the community. Our activities in and outside of the classroom brought together a wide variety of students from different cultural and socioeconomic backgrounds, and gave them a common goal to work toward. Our project also strengthened the relationship between the students, their families, the school, and the entire community. For some of the students, it was an opportunity to give back to the food bank, a place where their families have received help.

CiviConnections also contributed to the students' development of important work skills in planning, organization, and leadership, and contributed to their self-esteem. As one student commented, "Working at the AWARE Food Bank makes me feel like a better person." This program extended learning into the community and showed students that they can impact the community in a positive way. For many, it created what will hopefully result in a lifelong commitment to community involvement.

Various factors contributed to the success of our project. Strong administrative support from our building principal and the district office allowed us both curriculum flexibility and some financial backing. As mentioned earlier, Nancy Stone's leadership at the food bank proved to be essential. Our students' parents never made a negative comment or raised a concern; in fact, many were available to help as needed. We also recognize our own time and effort as critical to the project's success.

Yet without question, the efforts and dedication of a core group of students is the biggest reason for the success of this project. Woodburn's future will be better because of them. Their energy and enthusiasm were amazing and contagious. Our students grew to understand their responsibilities as citizens and to appreciate the power of their involvement.

In addition to the author, Kathleen Burd and Joseph Jensen were team teachers on this CiviConnections project.

⚜

Our Community, Our Responsibility: Food for Fowler

Sutter Middle School, Fowler, California

Monica Sigala

When we returned home from the CiviConnections summer workshop, our minds were buzzing with ideas for our small community of Fowler, California. We were eager to get our students to take part in a community-service project that would include a connection to our history standard. Would they accept the challenge? Would they be as passionate as we were? Each one of us looked through our history texts and pulled standards that would be possible links to community-service projects. Connecting community service to the social studies standards on ancient civilizations standards was a challenge, but we began with enthusiasm.

As part of our study of Meso-America and literature, we read an article by Anna Quindlen about poverty. This article set the stage for me to ask my students about issues in our own community. I presented the idea of service-learning and told them that their class would be involved in a project this year. All of the students began to ask many questions about community service. Each small group selected one student to make a list of three community-service ideas and share them with the class. I recorded the ideas on a large piece of butcher paper, noting repeated ideas with an asterisk.

The students generated many ideas, including a skate-park, an arcade, a new park, planting trees down Merced Street (our main street), a homeless shelter, and an animal shelter. As we viewed the list and considered our time constraints, we had to make a choice based on what would benefit our community immediately and how we could be a major force in taking action to help move our project along. Our discussion came down to two ideas: a skate-park (they were holding out hope for that one) and poverty. At the sixth grade and eighth grade levels, the same

activity took place, and they came up with a homeless shelter, an animal shelter, and a skate-park.

We then brought all ninety students together in the cafeteria to review the ideas. Student representatives researched each topic and presented their findings to the group. Afterwards, each of the three classes voted in our rooms, and everyone agreed that the issue of poverty was an area we could benefit most, although the skate park lingered in many minds.

In my class, the students worked in assigned groups on various activities. One group met with Mr. Gonsalves, who runs the Fowler Food Pantry out of his own home, with assistance from his wife and local church groups. Seeing the limited storage space Mr. Gonsalves had, the students quickly realized that more storage space was needed, as well as monthly donations that extended beyond the holiday season.

Another group began research to compare the ancient civilization of Meso-Americans to present-day society. More specifically, the students studied the social classes of the Olmec, the Maya, the Inca, and the Aztec. Each student chose one of these cultures and created a PowerPoint presentation that showed how each civilization treated its "poor" and working class. In each civilization, the peasant class built roadways, created pyramids, worked as servants, or became human sacrifices. My seventh graders compared their findings with the eighth graders' documentation of the poor and working class in U.S. history, highlighting child labor laws, railroad construction, the Great Depression, and the Dust Bowl. Students discovered that President Franklin Delano Roosevelt was one leader who actually put forth some effort to provide relief for those in despair.

A third group from my class studied present-day statistics. We learned that women and children were the most likely to be homeless in Fresno County. Earning less than $18,000 a year would place you at the poverty level, and in the year 2000, 180,000 people living in Fresno, California were considered poor. The class created PowerPoint presentations, posters, and skits based on their research.

After reviewing the facts from all three time periods, some students decided that although being poor during ancient times meant hard work or even death, at least having a "purpose" or a place in society would be a bit better than living on the streets alone. Other students countered that living a life on the street would be better than becoming a human sacrifice.

In preparation for the service aspect of our project, we invited three guest speakers to the class. Personnel from the Central Valley Food Pantry gave a 45-minute presentation outlining the need for donations year-round. The founder of the local homeless shelter gave a very moving and thought-provoking presentation, complete with video and books, causing many students to become outraged at the local statistics. Our last speaker was Mr. Gonsalves, who quietly spoke of his humanitarian efforts of the last 20 years. A retired police officer, Mr. Gonsalves thought nothing special of his work, saying it was the "human thing to do." The students decided that he and his wife should be recognized at our celebration.

The students decided we needed to revitalize the current food pantry. First, students created flyers listing the services the city of Fowler offers to those in need. With Mr. Gonsalves's permission, we listed his home address with the hours he accepts visitors. Students also felt it was important to list other government agencies and one local doctor and dentist.

Students placed food barrels at various locations in town. We were able to create a system with our local fire department where the site could call the Fowler Fire Department and one of the people on duty would pick up full barrels and take the food to the Fowler Food Pantry. We were able to collect over 2,000 items for our CiviConnections celebration! Today the barrels still exist at each site, and in November, the Sutter site collected close to 1,000 canned goods to donate to the pantry. Students also wrote letters to *The Fowler Ensign* sharing their project idea, the date of the open house/celebration, and inviting others in the community to make donations to the pantry.

In preparation for the celebration, students practiced skits and poems they had written. They ordered a plaque and a bouquet of flowers to present to Mr. and Mrs. Gonsalves. A formal invitation was sent out to the community of Fowler, including the school board, city council, parents of students, our administration, and local media. Small paper bags with a short description of our project were filled with donated items and an informational card to pass out at the celebration. Each paper bag carried a call to action (below).

The celebration was held in our multi-purpose building from 5:00-6:00 pm. Refreshments were served as invited guests watched a video of PowerPoint presentations about poverty in our community, in America, and through ancient civilizations such as Meso-America and Egypt. Students introduced the event with a welcome, followed by presentations of their skits, poems, illustrations, and reflections. After the students honored Mr. and Mrs. Gonsalves with a plaque of appreciation for their years of service to the community, we made some closing remarks, emphasizing the impact our CiviConnections project had on both our students and the community. While poverty has been on the planet for some time and will likely be around as long as there are human beings on earth, our students learned that we can all make a conscious effort to give to those who are less fortunate and to raise an awareness of poverty among our friends, families, and community.

In addition to the author, Brea McDonough and LeAnn Hodges were team teachers on this CiviConnections project.

Our Community, Our Responsibility: Sutter Middle School & Fowler Food Pantry
Together Making a Difference

The Fowler Food Pantry has been operated by Fowler citizen, Vernon Gonsalves. The pantry helps to provide food to hungry people in Fowler. Sutter Middle School has made it a priority to make sure the pantry never goes empty. It seems the number of people in need grows each year and we need to show our compassion through helping our community. We are the United States of America and it is important to unite together to address this issue. We can make a difference and leave behind a legacy that helps people, including children in Fowler. Sutter students will place barrels at various locations in Fowler and Malaga for donations.

Thank you for your support.

Rooms C-6, D-5, & C-3

Conclusion

Poverty is a critical issue in many communities in the U.S. and thus provides an appropriate focal point for a project. Investigating the local and national history of poverty leads to a wealth of data on how people's needs have been met (or not met). There are numerous hands-on activities students can then plan and carry out to meet the needs of those living in poverty in their own communities. All three projects in this chapter focused on providing food for those in need, in part through canned food drives. Yet the projects also illustrate the different ways that community partners, curricula, and student interests shaped project activities. Students in these programs worked at the food bank stocking shelves, wrote advocacy letters, held a rummage sale, placed barrels at community locations for food collection, and created both English and Spanish PR materials for a youth meals program. These effective service-learning activities reveal some of the varied and meaningful ways students can help their communities. ⬛

CHAPTER TEN

Poi to the World

Wai'anae Intermediate School, Wai'anae, Hawaii

LITIA HO

Native Hawaiians have one of the highest obesity rates in the nation, due primarily to the shift in their diets away from traditional foods such as poi (made from the taro plant, a main staple of the early Hawaiian diet) to burgers, french fries, and other "fast food." Recognizing the obesity and health-related crisis in their community, 120 seventh and eighth graders participated in "Poi to the World," a project aimed at educating teens and adults about the importance of eating healthy native foods.

As teachers, we wove the common threads of both our Pacific Island and American History units of study with the CiviConnections program objectives. We also integrated our dietary studies with several of Hawaii's content and performance standards. Under historical empathy, students learned to judge the past on its own terms and used that knowledge to understand present-day issues. In the area of Cultural Inquiry, students used the tools and methodology of social scientists to explain and interpret ideas and events. In the standard on Environment and Society, students demonstrated stewardship of the earth's resources.

The process of collecting data involved students in examining their Hawaiian history books, historical documents (such as the Social Security Act), and websites with health statistics. They were puzzled by their discovery that Hawaii is the fourth healthiest state in the nation, but the mystery was solved when they learned that Asians and Caucasians, not Native Hawaiians, are the healthiest residents. Further research involved students creating a questionnaire to distribute to school members, families, and neighbors. Students compiled their results and reported them to the class during math time. They also investigated a variety of local eateries and discovered that fast food "drive-throughs" were replacing older establishments.

Social studies lessons focused on various diet-related illnesses that affect young and old, as well as the historical background of how the overthrow of the Hawaiian monarchy transformed land ownership and how the change in agricultural lands affected the type of food grown and consumed. During a field trip to Hawaii's Plantation Village, hands-on activities enabled students to learn more about native fruits and vegetables. They also learned how many ethnic groups—Chinese, Japanese, Filipino, Korean, Portuguese, Puerto Rican, and Okinawan—served as the labor force on plantations, thus influencing the dietary habits of today.

With a focus on educating the community, service projects included an Open House Informational Booth, a Veteran's Day Community Booth, a Thanksgiving Canned Goods Drive, a Fall Fest Informational Booth, The Institute for Human Services Monetary Donation Drive (for nutritional meals), a Christmas Concert Informational Booth, and a Jamba Juice Literacy Campaign. Each activity was fully supported by our school administrators and staff, as well as many community partners. A highlight of our experience was being selected to present our project at both the National Service Learning Conference and the state of Hawaii service-learning conference. As young motivated citizens, our students volunteered their personal time during and outside of school to encourage a change in what people eat, why they eat, and how much they eat. Identifying viable ways to stop the cycle of obesity led our students to rethink the foods they eat and the amount they consume. "Poi to the World" made our students and our community aware of the consequences of their food choices. Hopefully many will shift their diets to native foods and live healthier lives in the coming years. 🐚

In addition to the author, Ada Maruyama and Karen Cole were team teachers on this CiviConnections project.

CHAPTER ELEVEN

Helping the Homeless

Rosemount High School, Rosemount, Minnesota

Thomas J. Scott and Rahima C. Wade

"My first thoughts going through my head are 'just don't stare.' Hopefully, she won't try to rob me," wrote a suburban ninth grader reflecting about a hypothetical scenario in which a homeless woman passes him on the streets of Minneapolis. What is most striking about this passage is its implicit assumptions: the homeless are thieves and they don't deserve to be acknowledged on the street. As teachers, we might find such attitudes callous and cynical; however, they convey a brutal honesty that many in society hold toward the homeless. From the perspective of the classroom, these attitudes pose several challenges. For example, in our current standardized-testing climate, is study of the homeless important enough to include in the curriculum? How do we adequately analyze a social group that is transient in nature, invisible to many Americans, and virtually powerless in a political and economic sense? Where do these units fit in the curriculum? Most important, how do social studies teachers address the stereotypes and cynicism held by many who live in "more fortunate" economic circumstances?

What follows is a reflection on these questions, informed by the first author's efforts to teach about homelessness and poverty to a group of middle and upper-middle class suburban ninth graders. From this reflective standpoint, curricular decisions are scrutinized, teaching methods are subject to critique, and student attitudes assessed. The result is a form of praxis: to create a framework whereby social studies teachers can take steps to reinvigorate our discipline; resist the current emphasis on a narrowing of the curriculum toward sterile, quantitative outcomes; and instill a heightened sense of relevance in which the social reality of our students' communities increases in prominence.

The Social Context

Dakota County has a per capita income of nearly $60,000 and is one of the wealthiest counties in Minnesota. It is a suburban milieu with tidy, well-manicured lawns and 3-car garages, located about 25 miles outside Minneapolis. Many of the students in the county have mothers and fathers with college degrees and well-paying jobs. In the midst of this affluence, however, a subaltern population exists that live in the shadows of wealth—predominantly women, many with children, often the victims of divorce, dead-end jobs, health-care emergencies, no insurance, addictions, and poor decision-making; they live on the margins of society outside the consciousness of typical suburban life. They are in many respects, invisible. According to census data, the number of poor residents in Dakota County rose 57 percent from 2000-2004, jumping from 12,757 to 20,028 people. Public Assistance cases were up 69 percent during this same time period.

It was in this dichotomous context that I chose to study homelessness in my Honors 9th grade American Government and Citizenship course, generously supported by a CiviConnections grant from National Council for the Social Studies. In addition to developing a variety of lessons dealing with poverty, the focus of the project was to link the students' local community to the formal curriculum through a service-learning project at a homeless shelter for women and children.

Student Perspectives on the Homeless

Prior to implementing the service project, I decided it was important to determine what general feelings and thoughts my four American Government classes had on the subject of homelessness. A reflective visioning exercise was given in which students wrote essays on the following scenario:

> You are walking down a street in downtown Minneapolis. Coming toward you is a young woman in her twenties, looking slightly disheveled, pushing a grocery cart full of blankets, shoes, and various bags. She is homeless. As she approaches, she looks up from her cart. What comes into your mind as she walks past you down the street?

From the students' reflective responses four themes emerged: plausible reasons for homelessness, objectification of homelessness, individual responsibility related to homelessness, and the lack of agency to address the issue as a social problem. Many students questioned how someone could become homeless and what their experience might be like. According to one student,

"I also start to wonder what made her like this, decisions she did or DID NOT make, or maybe she had a bad family background. Maybe her family didn't have enough money to send her to a good school. This lady could have dropped out of school so her parents cut off money supply. Maybe her parents were dead or she just doesn't have family."

Another student wrote,

"I wonder where she slept last night. I feel bad for her. She doesn't even have a place to live or even clean clothes. I wonder how she got the things she did, how long she's been on the street. I wonder what terrible things have happened to her."

Other students objectified homelessness, associating it with pity, empathy, fear, neglect, or scorn. In this regard, these students "blamed the victim" for her homelessness, suggesting that personal decisions like dropping out of school, conflict with family members, laziness, bad decision-making, theft, or substance abuse were the sole reasons why people become homeless. As one student wrote,

"I think that people shouldn't feel bad for her. She can walk, she can get a job. It's her own fault that she is homeless and cannot afford somewhere to live. It was probably a series of bad choices that left her homeless, but she could've prevented it and she could still fix it now."

Finally, several students expressed feelings of helplessness and lack of agency concerning how to solve the problem. One student remarked,

"You think, do I give them any money or do I just keep walking. Do I talk to them and say 'hello, how are you' or just keep walking. Do you offer them a place to stay for the night or just keep walking. All of these thoughts rush through your head, yet you have no idea in the world what to do."

Or as another noted, "there is not really much I can do for her because I am only 14."

Pedagogical and Curricular Challenges

It is clear from these reflections that most of the students had little understanding of the social, economic, or political dimensions of homelessness. Further, less than a handful had practical experience volunteering in homeless shelters. Many of the students saw homelessness as a confusing phenomenon and expressed frustration as to how they could possibly contribute to its solution.

The complex nature of the problem and the students' lack of agency pose significant challenges in constructing an appropriate curricular framework for the study of social problems like homelessness. Developing a suitable framework is complicated by standardized testing, as state-mandated tests tied to Federal guidelines such as the Adequate Yearly Progress (AYP) provision of No Child Left Behind legislation proliferate. There is significant pressure to narrow the dimensions of the curriculum so it conforms to easily identifiable quantifiable measures. For example, homelessness and poverty are not specifically mentioned in the 9-12 Government and Citizenship Standards or benchmarks created by the Minnesota Department of Education. The dilemma for many social studies teachers is clear: Do you risk an examination of community-based issues of social, economic, and political complexity that defy conventional curricular construction and assessment? Or, do you retreat to a "safe" curriculum driven by multiple-choice tests that ignore the social reality students experience in their communities?

Another challenge in developing a suitable framework for the study of social problems involves aligning units into the existing curriculum. Textbooks often ignore in-depth analyses of social issues. Finding resources for the study of homelessness, creating lessons, and integrating them in the appropriate context complicates curriculum alignment. For example, although my American Government curriculum did have a social justice focus, none of the units in the course analyzed homelessness or poverty. To overcome these curricular limitations, I provided my students with a variety of readings on the nature of poverty in the United States. We read and discussed an 1885 address delivered by Henry George, author of *Progress and Poverty*, from Howard Zinn and Anthony Arnove's *Voices of a People's History of the United States*. From the local county historical society, we acquired 19th century newspaper accounts of the "Poor Farm Movement," analyzing them in reading circles. We also read transcripts from Minnesota Public Radio of interviews with "inmates" who lived and worked on these farms throughout Minnesota. We viewed the PBS video "In this Affluent Society" to gain insights into attempts to alleviate poverty in the United

States under Lyndon Johnson's Great Society Program in the 1960s. We read and discussed the introduction to David Shipler's excellent book *The Working Poor: Invisible in America.* My students also undertook cooperative independent research to analyze the causes of poverty, how it is measured, the social and economic effects of poverty, and how poverty can be viewed from a global perspective.

The readings in particular elicited a variety of responses from my students about the nature of poverty in the United States. One important question we discussed and analyzed was why there is a general absence of narratives by the homeless and others who experience poverty. As one student remarked, "Those who usually write about poverty are not poor." Students recognized there was no proud heritage associated with being poor, as was true of a variety of other minority groups who had suffered historical marginalization in the U.S. Instead, the students felt the poor were often stigmatized. As one student noted "they don't want public recognition of their situation for fear they might be judged as failures." Another student recognized that poverty is "demeaning, swept under the rug by society, and very sad." Others noted that, "Many in poverty have given up hope. Who would read and who would care about their situation?" Comments like these have framed much of the discussion about poverty in the United States since the 19th century. Many of the students agreed that Henry George's view of poverty as a crime of society, an injustice in which "poor as well as rich, are responsible" has significant relevance in contemporary America.

Newspaper accounts of poor farms in Minnesota in the late 19th century were especially revealing. The accounts suggest that poor farm inmates fit a specific profile: most were male, many were physically infirm, some suffered from mental illness, others were alcoholics, and nearly all were indigent. In an obituary listing of poor farm inmates from a nearby township in the early 1900s, 14 of the 18 dead were immigrants, only two were women, and only one had an occupation as a baker.

During our discussions, one young woman stated, "There are so many impoverished people in the U.S., people accept them as normal. We don't view poverty as a form of oppression." Accounts the students read in a local community newspaper in 1893, however, attest to the oppressive nature of living on a poor farm. An inspection of the local poor farm (approximately 5 miles from our classroom) by the Secretary of the State Board of Corrections and Charities provides a shocking view of life for poor farm inmates. In his inspection, the Secretary noted: "The house is poorly built, with soft wood floors in a dilapidated condition... The broken condition of the plastering and the

shrunken condition of the wood work render it impossible to exclude vermin... There is no provision whatever for bathing paupers. During the past winter, eight male paupers have occupied a low chamber sixteen by twenty-one feet and seven and one-half feet high at the highest point... Seven of eight other men, crippled or infirm, occupied a room on the first floor, eighteen by twenty-one feet, and superheated by a large stove, without any provision for ventilation."

The primary source material and eyewitness newspaper accounts gave my students an insider's perspective on the historical nature of poverty that wasn't possible using conventional textbook instruction. Most important, my students gained important insights into the reality of those who have been marginalized by poverty, recognizing that the condition of being poor is complex and transcends personal responsibility.

An additional challenge involved preparing the students for a site visit at the homeless shelter. The civics curriculum must entail a symbiotic relationship between the school and the community. The social context of the community must be brought into the classroom, and conversely, the classroom must be taken into the community. The Executive Director of the shelter visited my ninth grade American Government classes as a guest lecturer, where she discussed the nature of homelessness in the county, the social stigma of homelessness, personal accounts of some of the women and children who had lived in the shelter, and the role nonprofit organizations play in addressing the problem of homelessness. The Executive Director's visit was followed by a student-run training session in which a group of 10th and 11th grade students, who had previously volunteered at the shelter, trained the 9th graders on practicing non-judgmental behavior, avoiding value-laden language and interacting appropriately with the children of homeless mothers.

Over a four-month period, 120 students visited the shelter, engaging in a variety of volunteer tasks such as reading to children, shoveling snow, discarding old mattresses, sorting the kitchen pantry, wrapping donated gifts for Christmas, sorting donated clothing, cleaning and sterilizing dining room tables and chairs, hauling donations, shredding documents, mopping hallways, organizing office files, making welcome tags, bagging clothes for other organizations, sanitizing children's toys, washing windows, disinfecting beds and dressers, and vacuuming floors. The students devoted nearly 360 hours of volunteer time that enabled the organization to enhance its direct services to residents.

The experiential learning associated with service projects is an essential part of developing a social studies framework related to the study of community-based issues. However, the service-learning project also presented several challenges. For example, the traditional seven-period day was a constraint because of students missing class, teachers' daily schedules being altered when a block of students were absent, and resistance to the project that emerged on the part of some teachers who felt it was not necessary to visit a site more than once. This was especially true of teachers in Math and English who were focusing on getting students prepared for the Minnesota Comprehensive Assessment.

It was also apparent that a disconnect emerged between the culture of the nonprofit with its flexible time frames and the regimented school culture with its rigid seven periods. The school schedule, in many respects, dictated the amount of time students spent at the site, and class size presented challenges to the nonprofit's staff as far as scheduling productive activities for thirty students. The Executive Director suggested at one point that 15 students volunteer per visit. However, this request was unrealistic from the school's perspective because of students' schedules, logistics related to staffing, and the supervision of students. Fifteen students was an ideal number of volunteers from the perspective of the Executive Director; it was a logistical roadblock from a classroom teacher's perspective.

An essential component of teaching community-based issues is a post-experience reflection. Such an exercise provided several purposes: it allowed students to cognitively process the concept of service as a form of community involvement and civic engagement; it allowed students to articulate the learning (or lack thereof) they received from engaging in service, and it provided a summative evaluation of the project from the students' perspective.

In late May, students once again wrote a reflective essay using the same scenario as they did in September. The question "How has your experience volunteering at the homeless shelter affected your view of homelessness?" was added to the exercise. Over 43 percent of the students wrote that the study of poverty and the service project led to a change in their views on homelessness. For example, they felt the project raised their awareness and created a deeper understanding of homelessness. As one student wrote,

> "My impression of homeless people after this year is totally different then it was at the beginning of the year. A while ago, I thought of homeless people as bums who didn't get work because they didn't try hard enough, but now I realize that they are just victims of poverty, and most of the time they are doing everything they can to get off the streets."

Another came to the conclusion that her stereotyped view of the homeless as lazy and dirty was wrong. She stated,

> "After going to the shelter I got a new sense of homelessness because when I picture someone homeless I see someone in rags and sitting on a street corner. But when I went to the shelter there were women and children in decent clothes and the mothers had jobs and were working hard. When I thought of homelessness I though of that person choosing to live on the streets and not working towards anything. At the shelter it was different from what I pictured and thought of homelessness. The shelter made me realize sometimes working hard doesn't get you where you need to go."

Many wrote that the homeless were not necessarily to blame for their situation, stressing that homelessness is a societal issue, not necessarily an individual one. Others noted homelessness is often caused by structural issues such as economic dislocation, low wages, or institutional racism. Several students began to see the homeless as normal people who deserved respect. These students argued we should be less judgmental of the homeless. In short, they saw homelessness as a much more complex problem than they had first imagined. The following quote illustrates this change in perspective:

> "I used to think homelessness was a choice or the result of a choice. Now, I understand that most times the person might have made a small choice but circumstances are to blame for many people in homeless situations. A lot of the time homelessness is the direct result of someone else's choices affecting the homeless person. Abusive/harmful relationships cause homelessness, along with addiction. Poverty along w/homelessness is often not an individual crime, but a societal crime. It's our responsibility to respond to the poor and homeless. Our responsibility i[s] a response to their individual situations."

Thirteen percent of the students responded that the experience did not effect any significant change of attitude toward the homeless. However, as the following quote suggests, many of these students also experienced a shift in their thinking. According to one,

> "I still have the same first thoughts when I see homeless people and though it may not be entirely their fault, I think they contributed to their situation. The shelter

didn't really change the way I see homelessness. I think they should go get jobs, and even though they may have jobs, I don't think it should be other people's responsibility to provide shelter for them. The shelter and the speaker did however make me realize that the homeless may be working harder than I thought."

Conclusion

As the post-reflection writing of students who participated in this service-learning project attests, engagement with the local community can produce powerful outcomes. A multifaceted curriculum, connected to the social reality of the community, presents students with a learning experience that enhances relevance and meaning in their lives. It provides them with a sense of engagement in their community, a chance to become active participants in addressing complex problems, and instills realism in the subject matter they study on a daily basis. Most important, service-learning tempers students' reliance on stereotypes to explain social phenomena. First-hand experience with specific societal problems may also reduce the hopelessness and disengagement many students associate with complex problems in society. It is our belief that service, in conjunction with a focused, realistic curriculum analyzing a specific community problem, will help students feel they can make a difference in the lives of others. This sense of agency is a powerful outcome that fulfills the ideals of citizenship and strengthens democracy.

The disconnect between community-based non-profits and schools, a curriculum dictated by standardized outcomes, and a pedagogy that focuses on facts rather than ideas are inter-related challenges that must be overcome to provide effective service-learning experiences for students. The first challenge, the institutional culture clash that can emerge between schools and nonprofit organizations that are dependent upon volunteers, is a significant dilemma. The differing needs and values in these two settings bring forth an important set of questions: What is a volunteer? What are the expectations of volunteerism from the school, and how do those expectations fit with the nonprofit organization? Can volunteerism be taught? Should the school teach the skills associated with being a good volunteer or should that be the job of the nonprofit?

The second challenge involves the constraints of the social studies curriculum. Ronald Evans has stated that one of the principal dilemmas faced by the social studies curriculum is "the failure of classroom practice to live up to the potential for interesting and engaging teaching worthy of the social issues we face as citizens."[1] As teachers, we are responsible for incorpo-

rating hundreds of subject-matter standards and benchmarks related to the social studies. Analysis of community-based issues often becomes an add-on, taxing our ability to find ways to integrate these issues meaningfully into the curriculum. The result, unfortunately, is that community issues often are ignored, and an important instructional element of citizenship is denied to many students. We agree with Harry Boyte when he states "Education should be practiced as a dynamic engagement with the world, its problems, and its work."[2] Seen in this light, a crucial element of the social studies curriculum must be the development of engaged citizens. But with the current educational focus on standardized testing, are social studies teachers compromising the historical mandate of the social studies to teach citizenship? What are the long-term consequences of the subordinate role citizenship education currently plays in American education? Is the development of citizenship skills being neglected in the pursuit of standardized test scores? Have standardized tests become more important in societal terms than the examination of community issues?

Finally, the pedagogical challenge requires teachers to take a risk and do things differently. In place of the current reliance on sterile teaching methods focused on quantifiable outcomes, social studies teachers must embed in their lessons the social reality of the community. Teaching that reflects realistic issues in the community will certainly impact the school culture. Instead of rigid, inflexible schedules, schools must re-conceptualize their institutional structures so that students have more flexibility to get involved with the communities in which they live. Instead of a curriculum of passivity and rote learning of factual information, the social studies curriculum must provide students the opportunity to engage in active learning where they can practice civic engagement skills such as critical thinking, oral deliberation skills, the capacity to detect bias and falsehood, problem solving, respect for difference, and tolerance for contending viewpoints, all of which are essential to a functioning democracy. Service-learning projects contribute to this vision of schooling—one in which schedules are flexible, students in a classroom can move independently rather than in a herd, and the curriculum is embedded, not only in social reality, but the pursuit of engaged citizenship.

To reinvigorate the social studies curriculum for the 21st century, social studies teachers must re-establish our discipline's historical commitment to instilling content and skills that produce active citizens. An interdependent relationship must be created between the curriculum, the school culture, and the community. What makes this relationship dynamic is the implementation of service-learning programs connected to community-based issues. The result is the creation of a more relevant, purposeful social studies, one that is committed to the principles of participatory democracy and the improvement of students' communities. 🖼

Notes

1. Ronald Evans, *The Social Studies Wars: What Should We Teach the Children?* (New York: Teachers College Press, 2004), 176.

2. Harry Boyte, *Everyday Politics: Reconnecting Citizens and Public Life* (Philadelphia: University of Pennsylvania Press, 2004), 118.

CHAPTER TWELVE

Grafton: The Town that Wouldn't Die

Taylor County Middle School, Grafton, West Virginia

Lynn Smith

Choosing an issue was easy for us, since our community was dying. Grafton had been an important railroad center since its beginning. However, in the 1970s and 1980s the railroad began moving services and personnel to other locations. From this point on, other businesses closed and the population decreased. The downtown area was beginning to look like a ghost town.

Community organizations began brainstorming ways to turn this downslide around. We thought if the students could learn about the history of their community and get involved in this process, they might continue to contribute as adults.

As we began investigating our community's history, students discovered their families' and neighbors' ties to the railroad. They eagerly conducted interviews, brought in pictures and materials from family storage (such as the booklet produced for Grafton's Centennial), and had many stories to share on a daily basis. Most of the instruction and research took place in social studies and language arts classes.

While exploring our nation's history, we learned that Grafton played an extremely important role. It was established in 1852, when the railroad put a line through, and became a communications center for the Baltimore and Ohio Railroad (B&O). Its significance increased during the Civil War, because of the railroad and its necessity for both the North and South. Our research uncovered many interesting tidbits for both teachers and students. One story we all enjoyed was about President Ulysses S. Grant's visit. Shortly after the war's end, he visited Grafton and tried to give a speech. Because sentiments were still high, one of the engineers kept moving an engine back and forth, so that Grant's speech could not be heard. The train came to a standstill, however, when a gun was held to the engineer's head so that Grant's speech could continue.

We had intended to explore the criteria for historical landmarks as part of examining government documents. However, our research concentrated on the historic buildings with which we were involved, and the important time periods in both Grafton's and the B&O's history. One building, the Merchants & Mechanics Savings Bank (M&M), has received historical

landmark status. Two community members worked with our students there. During the work periods they led tours, gave mini-lectures, and shared interesting facts about the building.

Our service-learning project focused on the revitalization of the downtown area. Our many community partners had more projects and ideas than we had time to do. Students cleaned and stacked bricks from a torn-down building that will be used for walkways. They also planted a perennial garden on the site of another torn-down building, with daffodils to spell out "GRAFTON." The third work project involved the restoration of the Merchants & Mechanics Bank. The Taylor County Historical Society had rescued many of the original wood fixtures. Our students sanded and cleaned, ripped up rotten flooring, and decorated for Christmas.

Coordinating many students to work effectively on these projects was not without its challenges. The first two weeks, students were on a rotating schedule for work sites; however, we found that some were not consistent in staying. At that point, we just put on the morning announcements what the day's work sites were. We also had some difficulties with weather situations. Since most of our work sites were outdoors, we could not work in the rain. We informed students that, if it was raining, we would move indoors to the M&M Building so that we did not lose work time.

The support of our community partners, other citizens, parents, and grandparents was overwhelming. Many worked side by side with us at our work sites. When we were sweltering in the heat, parents showed up with Popsicles or ice water. Then they donated hot chocolate as the weather turned cold. They brought their own tools or donated tools, gloves, and goggles.

For our community celebration, students produced a PowerPoint presentation, using digital pictures detailing our projects and showing them hard at work. The presentation also highlighted their community research. Students and parents provided refreshments with a railroad theme: rail mix (a chocolate-covered Chex mix), railroad ties (pretzel rods dipped in chocolate), McCrory's bricks (bar cookies), and broom cookies (representing cleaning at the M&M). The Taylor County Arts Council let us hold the celebration in a building they had renovated in the center of our work area. As hosts, the students welcomed our guests, showed the PowerPoint presentation, served refreshments, and guided visitors through the displays.

The major highlight of our CiviConnections project was the students' enthusiasm and positive attitude. Upbeat and frequent news coverage by our community newspaper, *The Mountain Statesman*, and the local television stations, Channel 12 WBOY-TV and Channel 5 WDTV-TV from Clarksburg, further enhanced our students' self-esteem. Many of these students had never been engaged in any type of service before.

In addition, our classes included special-education students who are physically, emotionally, and socially challenged. Their parents were especially appreciative of their children's efforts and our inclusion of them. As parents picked up their children, we usually received daily thanks. Grafton is not the same, now that our students have contributed their time to renovating the downtown area. We hope that these experiences in their youth will contribute to their continuing commitment as adults to improve our historic town. 🔳

In addition to the author, Nancy Ludwick and Pamela Cooper were team teachers on this CiviConnections project.

Of Jails and Jobs:
Toward Newberry's Economic Future

Newberry Middle School, Newberry, Michigan

Christine Harmon

Here is our recipe for a successful community service-learning project: Take eighty enthusiastic 7th graders. Stir regularly by three transplanted teachers who love the area in which they live. Sprinkle liberally and often with support and ideas from community leaders. The result? Student ownership in the economic future of their town.

In the past decade, our county has had some economic scares and setbacks. In the 1990s, the leading employer, a state mental hospital, closed its doors. Within 5 years, a prison facility opened on the old hospital grounds, becoming the third largest employer in the county. At the end of the last school year, community residents learned that the prison facility might close. Through pressure from a community grass roots campaign and an online petition, the prison was guaranteed funding by the state legislature. The threat of closure, however, remains a reality in the future.

This year we had another economic crisis. Our county's leading industry, logging, suffered a huge financial setback. The only railroad company owning the tracks through our region was refusing to send railcars to ship out our wood to paper mills and other buyers. Since no other company had permission to use the tracks, much of our raw material was decaying on woodlots, awaiting shipment. All of these events contributed to the focus for our CiviConnections project: to ensure the economic future of the Newberry community.

In order to understand the economic potential of our community, we researched its industrial history. At the Luce County Historical Museum, a wonderful group of volunteers led us through a tactile history of our area. Many students had no idea the building in the center of town was actually a museum! A postcard collector who lived in our community for many years, Jim Dwyer, presented over eighty poster-sized photos specifically highlighting the industrial beginnings of our community. Jim Dake, a life-long resident, shared about his early adult years

working in the charcoal plant. As they listened to and touched history, the students formed images with which to link data they would soon experience through their own research.

Digging into the economic past of our community, we read newspaper clippings describing the long-closed, pig iron plant which used iron ore from 100 miles away, charcoal from our area's wood supply, and limestone from surrounding areas. As students engaged in discussions about the changes in local industries, they discovered that our area had gone from a manufacturing hub to a raw material supplier for other businesses far away. Students compared Luce County with other communities dealing with economic changes. Studying communities surrounding closed iron ore mines nationally, even those that once supplied our pig iron plant, helped our students conceptualize successes and failures.

As the facilitators for this project, our goal was to get students thinking economically. In-class lessons and simulations introduced our students to terms like opportunity cost, supply, demand, entrepreneur, public, private, goods and services, cottage industries, industry, retail stores, natural resources, and allocation. Examining the U.S. Census Bureau's website of State and County Quick Facts for Luce County, MI, students were able to compile demographic data that led to an in-depth understanding of the local labor force. Other information, such as home ownership, showed the stability of those workers and their commitment to the community. Facts on population and income trends, crime rates, land area, and population density also contributed to students' understanding of the challenges at hand.

As students' knowledge and interest increased, we finally asked our guiding questions. What should Luce County do in order to survive through economic turmoil? What will save Newberry? Brainstorming led to discussions and heated debates. A wide range of ideas, from opening a shoe store or a mega mall to bringing in a huge factory, emerged. Several students thought that if it were easier for them to spend their money here in town, the economy would improve. That valid idea would be placed on the back burner. A larger camp of students was pushing for some type of industrial enterprise. They were beginning to see that our region's raw materials were leaving the area to be processed somewhere else. By creating finished products here in our area, we would then create more jobs for local people and ship out a valuable commodity. More money would be made and therefore stay in our community. In addition, when the threat of closures came, the economic base would not be one-dimensional. Luce County would be more able to bounce back than it is able to currently.

We asked what companies or products they could see being made in our county. We created a list of over 40 products. Through discussion and evaluation, the students narrowed the list down to seven different types of products. Researching these products led to a new intensity of activity in the classroom. In response to our explanations about doing product research, one student's eyes opened wide. "Mr. Griffis, you mean this is for real?" Student interest was furthered because they were working for a real goal important to them, their families, and their community.

In addition to sharing their findings with their classmates and teachers, students presented their best ideas with the local Economic Development Corporation. We also invited a local entrepreneur, Kevin Vanatta, to discuss what it takes to start a business in our area. His expertise was illuminating for all of us.

The First 7th Grade Economic Summit was attended by over 20 community leaders, EDC members, and interested parties. Our students, using PowerPoint, still photos, video clips, and sample products, revealed their suggestions for products that could be made in our area using our own raw materials. We weren't quite sure how 7th graders' ideas would be taken by these business and marketing professionals. Imagine our surprise when, during question-and-answer time, the members of their audience started discussing the products and asking questions! The visitors were impressed not only by the professionalism of the students, but also by the students' abilities and knowledge of the products' manufacturing processes and their viability for Luce County. While our students had suggested bringing in a new company from outside, the community leaders were quite interested in using our local business owners and resources. The adults were so charged by the students that they stayed and discussed the products long after the presenters had gone.

Technology has played a central role in our efforts. Assigning each student an individual e-mail account enabled them to easily share documents and projects with their partners for editing or revising. Even more valuable was the discussion board set up for the research portion of the project. A forum was assigned to each industry that students were researching. There they could post websites they found, share information with groups from other classes, and collaborate on their presentations. Using the Internet to research industries and census data, students were able to create slide show presentations for their final products.

Future plans include the students hosting and facilitating another meeting of local business owners and economic leaders, as well as developing a website, marketing CD, and book, which will help the Economic Development Council, Chamber of Commerce, employers, and real estate agencies promote Luce County for economic ventures, new residents, and tourists.

It might be very difficult to measure the success of our service-learning project. Perhaps some might call it a failure if our students aren't able to achieve our ultimate goal of bringing a new business to Newberry. But we know that our students' new knowledge of and investment in their economic future, along with the support and respect they generated in our community members and economic leaders, are a measure of success in their own right. Hopefully, our continuing collaboration will also lead to new jobs, industries, and businesses in our community. 🐚

In addition to the author, Cossondra George and Randall Griffis were team teachers on this CiviConnections project.

CHAPTER FOURTEEN

Volcano Safety for Senior Citizens

Kalles Junior High School, Puyallup, Washington
JEANNA KOOSER

"The Puyallup valley lies in the shadow of one of the top ten *most* dangerous volcanoes in the world. As we speak, thousands of unwitting residents of this and surrounding valleys are in great peril from a threat posed by the potential release of a thirty-foot wall of mud moving through the area." Melodramatic? Most definitely. Frightening? Perhaps not, unless one happens to be a resident of the suburban town of Puyallup, Washington.

The 7th grade students at Kalles Junior High School are greeted with these words as they view a video covering volcanoes that we use to introduce our geography and geology unit. The school is located, and our students live, in the Puyallup Valley in Washington State. This valley lies in the shadow of Mt. Rainier, one of the major mountains in the Cascade mountain range, part of the infamous "Ring of Fire." Through exhaustive research, geologists have determined that Mt. Rainier not only poses the standard threat of eruption, but notches up the peril by adding in the risk of a significant *lahar* (mud slide) spreading over our valley. Not only do scientists say this event has happened in the past, they indicate that a recurrence of a lahar is overdue. In layman's terms, this means that at some point (tomorrow, 100 years, 1,000 years), a large mudslide will release from the side of the mountain and cover the valleys below it. The threat is real enough that our school periodically practices four drills: intruder, earthquake, fire, and lahar. In case of a lahar the operative message to the over 50,000 residents of the valley area is "Get to higher ground… the sooner the better!"

After a long 'drill' day at my school (where we discussed the necessity for intruder, fire, earthquake, and lahar drills) we were struck by the number of incoming students who remained relatively ignorant of the threat that our scenic neighbor poses to us. For these reasons, we came to the conclusion that the development of a public awareness campaign would best meet the needs of our students.

Once our issue had been selected, we then turned to a more challenging aspect of the work. How could we incorporate the required elements of the project and remain true to our intent, while honoring standards-based learning? Our solution was to develop curricular projects that would satisfy the CiviConnections requirements and incorporate standards-based skills. We also decided to integrate Language Arts, and differentiate the projects to the degree that they could be used by both our special education and honors populations. Finally, we wanted to integrate a positive bent to our project. We did not want students focusing on just the negative elements of the mountain. We needed to balance the beauty and value of the mountain with the very real danger it presents.

Students participated in a variety of curricular projects on lahars and volcanoes. They created lahar maps (including historic elements and the likely path, speed, and coverage of a future lahar) and newspaper headlines detailing "research" evacuation areas, suggested evacuation items, and likely scenarios. The completion of these tasks required students to use primary and secondary source information. In addition, it pushed students to research a current issue. This project could not be completed without answers to such basic questions as: What is the problem? Who says it is a problem? Does anyone disagree? What is being done about the problem? Who is doing it? What have others done to examine the problem? All of these questions were posed as the project evolved.

Initially we thought it would be a struggle to incorporate government documents into our project, due to a perceived lack of access to materials and to the (somewhat) relative obscurity of the issue. We were happily surprised when our fire chief not only led us to government and historic documents relating to natural disasters, but also provided us with U.S. geologic society material directly related to our issue. In addition, our connection with the fire department ultimately helped us secure necessary funding for our project and helped us to more narrowly define our activities. Students were required to examine government documents when they completed work on their lahar tourist map and PowerPoint project (educational materials created by students which had to incorporate actual government evacuation plans). Students also had to access government documents, while researching government response plans, to create their realistic newspaper headlines.

The initial intent of the service aspect of our project was to create informative material for the community at large. Upon meeting with the local fire chief, we quickly discovered that senior citizens in our community were especially vulnerable to the threat of a lahar. Of the six nursing homes and assisted-living centers in our valley, none had developed evacuation plans. The fire chief was quite concerned about this situation. Once students were informed of the plight of our elderly neighbors, the issue took on greater relevance and concern. Ultimately, students visited these six homes and held a forum attended by 140 community members. Students shared information and supplies. Through the generosity of our fire department, we were able to donate a number of first aid kits. The concluding comments of our local fire chief said it best, "What you and your kids have done for this community, the entire Pierce County emergency management team could not have done without spending a lot more than the $1,300.00 we spent helping you. Plus, the connections kids were able to make were invaluable."

Our students received other recognition for their efforts as well. They were invited by the director of our county emergency management department to present on a local cable TV show, and the local newspaper covered our activities and interviewed some of the students.

Challenges we faced included development of "doable" lessons for our entire student population, balancing available resources, and logistical issues (transporting 300 students in shifts to six different homes, while finding coverage for classes). Creating lessons required a thorough examination of our curriculum and the availability of resources. The logistical elements fell into place because of the excellent rapport we were able to develop with our local fire department. The fire department had a need, and once we convinced them that our student population was very capable of filling this need, we received more support than we ever thought we would.

Overall, we consider our project to be a success. Students felt as though they contributed something that made a difference in the lives of local community members. Fire department and community members gained a much broader appreciation of the concrete contributions young people can provide if afforded the opportunity. What truly contributed to this project's success was the identification of a need, the willingness of a community institution to support the fulfillment of that need, and students' genuine interest in and connectedness to the issue. Finally, this project was solid evidence that even in a community where standards-based curriculum and a very set scope and sequence exist, service-learning can flourish.

We proudly display our student-created evacuation route at our school, and use the student-created PowerPoint presentation to educate incoming students about this continued hazard to our community. CiviConnections allowed us to venture into this terrain and evolve our curriculum beyond the ominous announcement that our grand volcano is one of the "top ten dangerous volcanoes in the world!" Students left this project feeling empowered and informed, having contributed to addressing this very real community issue. 🔊

In addition to the author, Dessie Evans and Nicole Greenwood were team teachers on this CiviConnections project.

CHAPTER FIFTEEN

Bridging the Years:
An Intergenerational History Project

Shenandoah Elementary School, Orlando, Florida • Princeton Public School, Princeton, Wisconsin
Rahima C. Wade, Diane Gardner, Paul Doro, and Sandy Arendt

Billy is a nine-year-old in a fourth grade class at a suburban Florida elementary school. As the oldest of four children with no male role model at home, Billy only makes it to school a few days a week. On the day the class was scheduled to visit the local senior assisted-living residence, Billy announced that the project was a "stupid waste of time" and frankly, he would rather be back in class "doing times tables."

But as luck would have it, Billy was paired up with Hank, an 89-year-old retired fighter pilot for the U.S. Air Force. Billy sauntered into the senior's room with a sulk on his face and hands in his pockets. He did not want to be there.

"Hey, you comin' in or staying out? I haven't got all day, ya know," chided Hank. "Well, actually I do 'cause I'm not going anywhere." This made Billy smile.

"How old are you?" Billy queried.

"I'm old enough to be your daddy's grandfather," Hank responded proudly.

"I ain't got a daddy," Billy noted in a matter-of-fact way. At this point, Billy's teacher, Diane, left the pair to their own devices and worked her way around the care center, matching the rest of her class with their senior "buddies." When it was time to go back to school, the fourth grade teachers began to round up their students. While taking a head count, Diane realized that Billy was missing. Her heart sank. She was so busy monitoring students and moving around that she had forgotten to go back and check on Billy and Hank. "This could be bad," she thought, as she raced to Hank's room. The door was only slightly ajar. She nervously pushed it open and saw Billy sitting in front of Hank, watching him as he raised his tattooed arms over his head to demonstrate a flight he had taken in a fighter jet. Billy's eyes were as big as saucers. Hank's face was lit up like a Christmas tree. She hated to interrupt them, but their bus was about to leave. These two friends, 80 years apart, had a very difficult time parting. Finally, totally unexpectedly, Billy wrapped his arms around Hank's neck and gave him the biggest hug Diane

had ever seen. It took her breath away.

At first glance, a nine-year-old child may seem to have little in common with an 89-year-old senior. Yet the connection Billy and Hank found in their budding friendship is seen around the globe—it is the connection formed between grandparents and their grandchildren, elderly residents and their young neighbors, and village elders and youth in tribal settings.

While the intergenerational bonds remain strong for children with elder relatives living close by, increasingly children in the U.S. lack meaningful connections with older adults. Divorce and family mobility are two major causes, and some youth are affected by negative stereotypes of older people.[1] Bringing seniors into our classrooms, or taking students to places where older adults live, can help to fill this social and emotional gap in many young people's lives. As social studies teachers, we can bring some of the benefits of intergenerational relationships to our students, providing many benefits for seniors and motivating children to become excited about the social studies curriculum. This article focuses on the many benefits of intergenerational social studies activities for children and seniors, and a variety of ideas for developing intergenerational activities to enrich elementary social studies instruction.

Everyone Benefits

Successful intergenerational activities provide rewarding experiences for both generations. Seniors share their skills and life experiences, dispel negative stereotypes of the elderly, and create meaningful friendships at a time in their lives when they are often losing friends and relatives or watching their physical capabilities diminish. Youth gain first-hand knowledge of the past, broaden their understanding of aging, and learn to accept

This article has also been published in the NCSS journal for elementary educators, *Social Studies and the Young Learner* 19, no. 3 (January-February 2007): 24-28 differences among people. Working together, youth and elders can pool their resources to build a stronger social network in their community, connect with social agencies, broaden the life experiences of both populations, and facilitate students' learning of social studies topics.

Paul and Sandy's fourth grade students found a gap they could fill at the King Veteran's Home in King, Wisconsin. Many of the war veterans living at the King home felt alienated from the rest of their community, largely because of the isolated location of their residence. After meeting with both administrators and veterans living at the home, the elementary students engaged in a variety of shared activities, from letter writing and visiting the seniors, to cleaning the library, making banners with uplifting messages, and coordinating an intergenerational dance. Students also performed patriotic programs and collaborated with their older friends on a craft project. The culminating activity for the year saw King residents (the ones who were physically able) bussed to the elementary school for an intergenerational celebration with dances, snacks, and shared conversation.

The intergenerational collaboration also provided the elementary students with meaningful opportunities for learning social studies content. Paul and Sandy helped their students read the Preamble to the Constitution of the American Legion, discuss the vocabulary, and consider how to relate these terms to their daily lives. Each group used dictionaries and artwork to create a poster about a different aspect of the preamble; helpfulness, democracy, peace, and goodwill were some of the topics. Older students used the Internet to investigate the charter documents and the initial purposes of several organizations, including the American Legion, the Veterans of Foreign Wars, the Daughters of the American Revolution, and the King Veterans Home.

Elementary students also conducted a hands-on investigation of U.S. history while exploring the cemetery across the street from the King home. Their challenge was to find time-related data on the headstones, from all eras of history since the Civil War. Students particularly enjoyed searching for, and discovering, the gravesite of Brownie, a dog that had served in the Canine Corps during World War II.

Links with the Curriculum
The lessons on the documents of citizen organizations and U.S. history from Paul and Sandy's classrooms are just one example of how elementary social studies teachers can integrate youth and elderly collaborations to motivate young people's engagement with the social studies curriculum. Diane and her fourth grade colleagues, Nancy and Allison, focused on a history of social

service. Their students interviewed the care center residents about how they helped out and made a difference in each other's lives when they were young, thus providing the fourth graders with additional ideas for how they can help their community. Students could perceive how their community's needs, problems, and social service system had changed over time. Students developed their interview questions together during writing workshop time. Examples were: "What sport or activities did you enjoy in your childhood?" "What chores did you have to do to help your parents?" "Can you remember a time when you helped others?" "Is there some service that you wish could be provided for you here at the assisted living center?"

The students also were interested in taking civic action on behalf of the seniors as part of their social studies lessons back at school. The last question on their interview sheet read: "We are learning about our local, state, and federal government this year. I would like to be an advocate (a person who wants to speak on your behalf) for you by writing a letter to a public official concerning your needs as a senior citizen in America (for example, on the topic of healthcare, social security benefits, etc.). Is there any issue that concerns you now that you would like me to advocate for you?" This question led to several opportunities for further learning and letter writing.

Specific Topics
Consider the following additional ideas for incorporating intergenerational sharing in your social studies curriculum:

ORAL HISTORIES: Students can interview seniors on a variety of topics in their life experience, for example, schooling, games, foods, careers, community development, and civic organizations. (See the interview ideas in the Handout.) Or students can interview seniors about a significant historical event they are studying—such as the Great Depression or the Civil Rights Movement—to gain further insight into how these events have influenced daily life.

INTERGENERATIONAL SERVICE LEARNING: Students and seniors can work together to meet community needs. For example, they could sew quilts for babies, create alphabet books for Head Start pre-school students, build birdhouses, or create a meal for a local soup kitchen.

COMPUTER PROJECTS: Students can teach seniors how to use the Internet and simple programs such as PowerPoint. Together, they can research a social studies topic and create a presentation for the class or community, and maybe videotape the presentation for airing on a local television show.

FIELD TRIPS: Seniors can serve as field trip "guides" to community locations or historical sites, providing additional adult supervision and perhaps insights from their own life experience.

PRIMARY SOURCES: Elders can often provide primary sources from earlier time periods that will enrich young students' learning of history—letters, journals, clothing, uniforms, postcards, and other memorabilia can give students insight into the recent past.

GLOBAL STUDIES: Students can learn about other countries and cultures from seniors who have traveled or lived abroad. Immigrants to your community can be a rich resource of knowledge of other cultures and places.

FAMILY HERITAGE: The elementary social studies curriculum typically includes units on family or activities on family heritage. Seniors can share the legacy of their families with the class and assist young students with unit activities, such as constructing a family tree.

To insure that your intergenerational activities are supportive of your social studies curricular goals, align discussions or interviews with the NCSS thematic strands (Figure 1).

Building a Relationship

The fourth-grade team from Florida included art projects in their intergenerational program. Students took photos of their senior buddies and conducted interviews with them about how they had served and helped others in their lives. With the purchase of scrapbook materials through their CiviConnections grant,[2] the students created scrapbooks of their senior buddies' lives to present to them. Subsequent class visits built upon the success of Diane's earlier activities. On one visit, the older adults were waiting for the students in the cafeteria. They could not contain their excitement. The students came rushing in, searching the faces to find their senior buddy. Carly ran to Ms. Rose and practically sat on her lap! With a child's arms wrapped around her frail neck, Ms. Rose went on and on about how much she loved her "girl."

In two weeks, we will be visiting the assisted-living center to conduct our celebration. Balloons are on order and the children have volunteered to make all of the baked goods. We've asked the director to give us the name of some large-print books and music that the seniors might enjoy as a donation from our students. Everyone is very excited about this "last visit," but we hope that students won't really make this their last visit. At least

Figure 1. Intergenerational Activity Ideas and Studies Thematic Strands

❶ CULTURE
Learn about seniors' home cultures, or cultures of places where they have lived or visited.

❷ TIME, CONTINUITY, AND CHANGE
Explore the changes in schooling, play, lifestyle, community, etc., from when seniors were young until the present.

❸ PEOPLE, PLACES, AND ENVIRONMENTS
Talk about how the environment has changed over seniors' lives. Mark on a map where seniors have traveled and lived.

❹ INDIVIDUAL DEVELOPMENT AND IDENTITY
Explore the key influences on seniors' individual development from youth to adulthood.

❺ INDIVIDUALS, GROUPS, AND INSTITUTIONS
Discuss how schools, churches, families, and other societal groups and institutions have changed.

❻ POWER, AUTHORITY, AND GOVERNANCE
Talk about when seniors first voted, what elections they remember, and their perceptions of changes in government.

❼ PRODUCTION, DISTRIBUTION, AND CONSUMPTION
Learn about how products and prices have evolved over time. Talk about what items we use today that did not exist when seniors were young. Consider changes over time in options for jobs and careers.

❽ SCIENCE, TECHNOLOGY, AND SOCIETY
Students and seniors could come up with a list of the Top Ten scientific discoveries and technological inventions that have most significantly changed society in the past century.

❾ GLOBAL CONNECTIONS
Talk about how seniors learned about the world when they were young, and compare that with children's experiences now.

❿ CIVIC IDEALS AND PRACTICES
Explore how seniors were involved in their neighborhoods and communities as youth and young adults, and contrast these experiences with the options for youth today.

Student (Interviewer) _____ Date_____

Older Adult (interviewee) _____

---

1.   When and where were you born?

2.   Who was in your family?

3.   What was your elementary school experience like?

4.   Who was your favorite teacher?

5.   What was your favorite subject?

6.   What games did you play?

7.   How did you spend your free time?

8.   What chores did you have at home?

9.   When did you get your first job?

10.   Where did you live as an adult?

11.   Did you work as an adult? If so, what did you do?

12.   Where have you traveled?

13.   What has been most important to you in your life?

14.   What advice for living a happy life do you have for children today?

two students have visited their senior buddies on a Saturday, on their own volition.

"I had nothing to do and then I thought of my senior buddy and how lonely she must be. I asked my mom if we could stop by on the way to the store and she said, 'Yes!'" explained one of my students. This is the best example of a motivated student, one who seeks additional experience on her own.

Planning Checklist

There are many more stories we could tell about how motivated elementary students become when they work with older adults. Planning ahead is important for a successful experience. These elements are essential for creating positive intergenerational collaborations:

Involve youth, seniors, and personnel from senior care centers in planning the collaboration so that everyone's needs and interests are met, in addition to the teacher's. You might begin by writing a letter to send home to your students' parents, informing them of the collaboration and inviting their input, as well as permission for and assistance with transportation. A planning meeting between seniors and children could happen either at the school or at a local residence for older adults.

Prepare youth and seniors before they get together. They need to know what to expect in terms of each other's physical abilities, attention spans, interests, and conversation skills. Staff at the residence might be able to come to your classroom to inform students about the mental and physical capabilities of the particular group of older adults with whom they will be working. You and your students could also take a preliminary tour of the senior facility.

Engage students and seniors in meaningful activities. Generations Together, a longtime intergenerational program based at the University of Pittsburgh, notes that "It is

not just enough to bring people together. They have to have something worthwhile and appropriate to do together."[3] Meaningful activities will accomplish at least three goals:

1. Meeting the companionship and self-esteem needs of the seniors.
2. Providing enjoyable cross-age interaction for children.
3. Incorporating social studies content and skills in the experience.

One activity that meets all three goals is to have students interview seniors about their lives and create a book of the biographies to give back to the seniors.[4]

Intergenerational friendships can provide a "real-life" connection to the study of history, extra hands of adult volunteers for in-class activities, and an opportunity for students to provide companionship for their elderly neighbors. With so many possible connections to the social studies curriculum and so many benefits for both elders and youth, we hope you will consider an intergenerational activity for your students soon.

Notes

1. Lorine Matters, *Intergenerational Relations: Older Adults and Youth. County Extension Program Guide* (Columbia, MO: Missouri University Center on Rural Elderly, 1990).

2. CiviConnections is a program for 3rd through 12th grade classrooms to link local historical inquiry with community service-learning. It is funded by National Council for the Social Studies, with support from the "Learn and Serve" program of the Federal Corporation for National and Community Service. Training will be offered during July 2007. For further information, contact the project director, Rahima Wade, at rahima-wade@uiowa.edu.

3. Generations Together, *Share It with the Children: Preschool Curriculum on Aging Instructional Guide* (Pittsburgh, PA: University of Pittsburgh, 1990): i.

4. Alison Parker, "Visiting and Interviewing Older Adults: Service-Learning in the Sixth Grade," *Middle Level Learning* 15 (September 2002): 3-7.

CHAPTER SIXTEEN

Panthers for Pages

Perry Local Schools, Massillon, Ohio

KATHY STEELE

Three years ago, the Perry Branch of the Stark County Library was completely destroyed by fire. It was arson, which made the loss of the library even more devastating to our community. The library was central to most of the schools in the district, nestled between the junior high school, the middle school and the high school. As a result, many of our students were able to walk to the library for work on papers, school projects, computer use and the like. Because Perry is primarily a blue-collar community, our students relied on the library for technology that they might not have available to them within their own homes. The loss of this facility seriously impacted the students and their ability to access tools necessary for their education. When we contacted Mrs. Dick, the head of the Perry Branch Library, we discovered that she was very excited about working with us and our students. Thus, our project, "Panthers for Pages," (our school mascot is the panther) was born!

The first few weeks were devoted to researching and chronicling the rebuilding efforts of the new library. The kids looked at prior programming in the community and Perry's demographics in order to understand what the library's focus was and how its staff went about determining the resources and programs that would be available to students and their families. A brainstorming session produced many fun and creative ideas to raise funds for the Perry Branch facilities and programming. While it was a challenge to coordinate efforts between students at both the middle and high schools, they were very excited about getting started as soon as possible.

During our historical investigations, students discovered information on the origins of libraries here in the United States, including the contributions made by Benjamin Franklin and Thomas Jefferson to our first great libraries. For example, our students enjoyed looking at Thomas Jefferson's will detailing the donation of his extensive collection of books to begin the most impressive library in our nation—the Library of Congress. We also looked at the evolution of libraries and the historical importance of the Presidential libraries. In our explorations of library funding, many of the students were surprised that our

local library system has tax levies and that without that source of funding, the library would not be able to operate.

The most exciting part of our partnership with the library came through the fund-raising events that we held to raise money for programs, books, DVDs, and technology equipment. Most of the funds were spent to benefit the Teen Library Section. The new library has a specific area set aside for teens that includes a fireplace, seating that is computer compatible, a project room designed for spreading out and working on group assignments, and a beautiful deck that overlooks Sippo Lake with comfortable furniture for studying and relaxing with a good book! The library is also putting together some excellent new programming, addressing issues that affect teenagers during their most challenging years.

Our first fundraiser was a Read-a-Thon. Students asked their families and friends to sponsor them for a specific amount per page or a flat fee. Working in teams of three or four, someone from each team had to be reading at all times for the duration of the 9-hour, overnight Read-a-Thon. When students were not reading, teachers and parent chaperones supervised other activities. While the library was reserved for reading, in the gymnasium we had volleyball, ping pong, basketball and air hockey available. In the cafeteria we showed movies and played cards and board games. Local businesses donated pizza and pop. The Read-a-Thon was a great way to kick-off our program. Sixty students had fun and raised $1,000.00. We had no problems throughout the night; everyone was diligent about taking their turn at reading, although it became increasingly difficult to keep one's eyes open in the early morning hours! Additional fundraising efforts—a bake sale and penny collection—netted another $845 for the library.

Our last fund-raising event was a Silent Auction at our community's "Perry Fun Day." High school students helped get donations for the auction from local businesses and services. Junior high school kids prepared library displays and sat at the booths during the auction. With persistence, we managed to get over 36 donations including dinners from local restaurants, golf passes from top golf courses in the area, Cleveland Indians tickets, spa packages, a quilt, a wonderful family basket from the library and a 6-week old puppy from one of the breeders in the area. The auction was very exciting. We started the bids at 9:00 a.m. and closed out the bids at 1:00 p.m. We had people crowded around each donation waiting until the last minute to make sure that they got in the last bid for the item they wanted. Most of the people collected their items and paid for them at that time. We had about four items that we had to collect after that Saturday, but all money is in now and the total for our auction was $1,100.00! The students and teachers did a wonderful job in their presentation and decoration for the auction and put in many hours to have a successful event.

Our students are still doing volunteer hours at the library, assisting with children's story hours, helping senior citizens and doing paperwork. They are also going to have a tile painting project on a Saturday morning for younger children. Each child will pay $5.00 to paint their favorite story book character on a tile. The tiles will be glazed and then will form the main wall of the Children's Library in the new building.

Of course, no service-learning project is without its challenges. The major ones we faced were scheduling (meetings between teachers, students' after-school conflicts) and time (there were several activities we simply did not have the time to complete this year). But overall, our students did a wonderful job in carrying out our service-learning goals. The project's success is due to the dedication of the students and teachers involved, as well as the cooperation of our wonderful library staff, school administrators and parents, who pitched in as needed on many occasions.

The Perry Branch of the Stark County Library opened on May 10, 2007. The official opening has been scheduled to take place at a later date. For this grand opening, Mrs. Dick has invited us to put together some displays for their new showcases to document our service-learning journey. Featuring the photos taken at each of our events, these displays will show the progression of our efforts to create a new library for our students and the community. As a result, the students and teachers in the Perry Local Schools will know that many of the wonderful books, programs, and facilities are in place because of their commitment to this service-learning project. 🔊

In addition to the author, Elizabeth Regula and Hope Lentz were team teachers on this CiviConnections project.

Conclusion

Conclusion

What if every student in our middle and high schools in the U.S. had the opportunity to participate in at least one CiviConnections project as part of their social studies courses? Not only would they have the types of memorable experiences recounted by teachers in this Bulletin, but they might also contribute to a revitalization of civic involvement among youth. This could in turn lead to stronger participation in the social and political life of their communities when they become adults. According to the students themselves, participation in a CiviConnections project has led to important changes in attitudes and skills. Participants have learned how to investigate the community and work with community members, and they have significantly increased their intent to serve their communities in the future.[1]

What has made CiviConnections work for students as an effective civic education program? In analyzing the many stories teachers have shared in this Bulletin and in program evaluation measures (e.g., final reports, interviews, and questionnaires) it seems that their success can be attributed to what I will call the "3 Cs": creativity, critical thinking, and collaboration. Let's consider each of these in turn.

First, CiviConnections projects have, without a doubt, been creative efforts on the part of teachers, students, and community members. While the six steps provide a framework for the creation of a project, there has been no scripted curriculum or exact set of procedures that can be followed. As with any high-quality service-learning experience, students and teachers, with community input, have designed site-specific experiences that were unique to their needs and interests. Creativity has been evident throughout the CiviConnections steps, from the need to fit the project with standards-based curricular requirements, to the many forms of service and advocacy that students planned and implemented. Teachers have exercised creative thinking in involving large numbers of students in service experiences, in communicating across grades levels and schools, and in finding time during (and occasionally outside of) the school day to plan and implement the program. Students have developed their creative-thinking skills as they sought out appropriate resources

to learn about the community's history, devised plans for how to make significant contributions to their community, and produced presentations and displays to celebrate their service and inform community members of their efforts.

Second, CiviConnections projects have involved critical thinking about social and environmental issues. They have demonstrated how an individual can best make a difference on a selected issue. For many students, the initial process of choosing an issue required critical thinking as they brainstormed and evaluated alternatives and selected the most appropriate problem to address. And as students considered various and sometimes conflicting sources of data during their local historical inquiry, they had to think critically about the sources of these data and whose stories were being told or left out. Perhaps most importantly, the heart of the CiviConnections experience has been about asking critical questions such as the following: What is wrong here? What needs changing? What has been tried and why hasn't it worked? The foundations of the CiviConnections program have been a willingness to question the status quo, and to take a critical look at the problems in our democracy and how we can live differently with each other in ways that support everyone's needs.

The third "C," collaboration, is perhaps the most visible of the three keys to success. It exists on many levels: teachers collaborating with each other to involve their students in high-quality service-learning, students collaborating with each other to implement project activities, and, of course, teachers and students both collaborating with community members, from the investigation phase through the community celebration. Notably, the teacher authors repeatedly credit their local community partners, and the support and affirmation they provide to students, as instrumental to the success of their projects. The best CiviConnections projects have truly been team efforts in which everyone is serving and learning.

While CiviConnections has largely been focused on students learning about (and serving) the community, one gets the sense that the community is also learning about the youth in its midst.

Several teachers noted that their students' participation in the life of the community led to changes in how community members viewed youth. The local fire chief, the director of the food bank, the area news reporter, the local business owners—these and other individuals in several of the chapters here evidenced surprise at both the interest and capabilities of young people. CiviConnections projects have addressed a wide variety of community problems, yet almost every project has also addressed the same need in communities across America—to close the divide between young and old, and simply to build a more cohesive and supportive community.

Bringing youth and adults together in positive ways for mutual benefit is a promising start. Yet we have a long way to go to create an equitable and just society in which the majority of our citizens participate in the social and political life of our democracy. Projects like those of CiviConnections are not a panacea, and any community collaboration addressing long-term social and environmental issues will face significant challenges and shortcomings. Yet the program can serve as a viable step in our journey as social studies educators to give our students the opportunity to put social studies to work in the community, and to learn firsthand the purpose and value of civic participation. CiviConnections has been exciting to many students because, as one said, it's "for real." Through hands-on research focused on real and present community problems, students learn and serve, bringing new meaning to both the life of the community and the civic goals of social studies education.

Note

1. For in-depth research results on student outcomes (knowledge, skills, attitudes, and intent to serve) of the first year of the CiviConnections program, see Rahima Wade and Donald Yarbrough, "Service-Learning in the Social Studies: Outcomes of the 3rd-12th Grade CiviConnections Program," *Theory and Research in Social Education* (in press).

Selected Resources on Service–Learning, Historical Inquiry, and Civic Education

Alliance for Service Learning in Education Reform (ASLER). *Standards of Quality for School-Based Service-Learning.* Chester, VT: ASLER, 1993.

Anand, B., M. Fine, T. Perkins, D. Surrey, and the Renaissance School Class of 2000. *Keeping the Struggle Alive: Studying Desegregation in Our Town.* New York: Teachers College Press, 2002.

Apple, M., and J. Beane, eds. *Democratic Schools.* Alexandria, VA: ASCD, 1995.

Barber, B. *Strong Democracy: Participatory Politics for a New Age.* Berkeley: University of California Press, 1984.

Barton, K. C., and L. S. Levstik. *Teaching for the Common Good.* Mahwah, NJ: Erlbaum, 2004.

Battistoni, R. M. *Public Schooling and the Education of Democratic Citizens.* Jackson: University Press of Mississippi, 1985.

Battistoni, R. "Service-Learning and Civic Education." In *Education for Civic Engagement in Democracy: Service-Learning and other Promising Practices*, edited by S. Mann and J. J. Patrick. Bloomington, ID: ERIC Clearinghouse for Social Studies/Social Science Education, 2000.

Beane, J., J. Turner, D. Jones, and R. Lipka. "Long-Term Effects of Community-Service Programs." *Curriculum Inquiry* 11 (1981): 143-155.

Becker, T. L., and R. A. Couto. *Teaching Democracy by Being Democratic.* Westport, CN: Praeger, 1996.

Beyer, L. E., ed. *Creating Democratic Classrooms: The Struggle to Integrate Theory and Practice.* New York: Teachers College Press, 1996.

Bellah, R. N., R. Madsen, W. M. Sullivan, A. Swidler, and S. M. Tipton. *Habits of the Heart: Individualism and Commitment in American Life.* New York: Harper and Row, 1985.

Billig, S. H. "Research on K-12 School-Based Service-Learning: The Evidence Builds." *Phi Delta Kappan* 81 (2000): 658-664.

Billig, S., S. Root, and D. Jesse. *The Impact of Participation in Service-Learning on High School Students' Civic Engagement.* Denver, CO: RMC Research Corporation and Center for Information and Research on Civic Learning and Engagement (CIRCLE), 2005.

Blythe, D., R. Saito, and T. Berkas. "A Quantitative Study of the Impact of Service-Learning Programs." In *Service-Learning: Applications from the Research*, edited by A. Waterman. Mahwah, NJ: Lawrence Erlbaum, 1997.

Boyle-Baise, M. "Community Service-Learning for Multicultural Education: An Exploratory Study with Pre-service Teachers." *Equity and Excellence in Education* 31, no. 2 (1998): 52-60.

Boyle-Baise, M. *Multicultural Service-Learning: Educating Teachers in Diverse Communities.* New York: Teachers College Press, 2002.

Chi, B. S. *Teaching the 'Heart and Soul' of Citizenship: Service-Learning as Citizenship Education.* Unpublished Ph.D. dissertation, University of California, Berkeley, 2002.

Conrad, D. "School-Community Participation for Social Studies." In *Handbook of Research on Social Studies Teaching and Learning*, edited by J. P. Shaver, 540-548. New York: Macmillan, 1991.

Conrad, D., and D. Hedin. "School-Based Community Service: What We Know from Research and Theory." *Phi Delta Kappan* 72, no. 10 (1991): 754-757.

Dewey, J. *Democracy and Education.* New York: The Free Press, 1916/1966.

Dewey, J. *Experience and Education.* New York: MacMillan, 1938/1963.

Ehrlich, T. "Civic Education: Lessons Learned." *PS: Political Science and Politics* 32, no. 2 (1999): 245-250.

Engle, S., and A. Ochoa. *Education for Democratic Citizenship: Decision Making in the Social Studies.* New York: Teachers College Press, 1988.

Eyler, J. "Stretching to Meet the Challenge: Improving the Quality of Research to Improve the Quality of Service-Learning." In *Service-Learning through a Multi-Disciplinary Lens*, edited by S. H. Billig & A. Furco. Greenwich, CT: Information Age Publishing, 2002.

Eyler, J., and D. E. Giles, Jr. *Where's the Learning in Service-Learning?* San Francisco: Jossey-Bass, 1999.

Fendrich, J. *Ideal Citizens*. Albany: State University of New York Press, 1993.

Ferguson, P. "Impacts on Social and Political Participation." In *Handbook of Research on Social Studies Teaching and Learning*, edited by J. P. Shaver, 385-399. New York: Macmillan, 1991.

Freire, P. *Pedagogy of the Oppressed*. New York: Continuum, 1970.

Galston, W. A. "Political Knowledge, Political Engagement, and Civic Education." *Annual Review of Political Science* 4 (2001): 217-234.

Gastil, J. *Democracy in Small Groups: Participation, Decision Making and Communication*. Philadelphia: New Society, 1993.

Giles, D., E. P. Honnet, and S. Migliore. *Research Agenda for Combining Service and Learning in the 1990s*. Raleigh, NC: National Society for Experiential Education, 1991.

Guarasci, R., and G. H. Cornwell. *Democratic Education in an Age of Difference: Redefining Citizenship in Higher Education*. San Francisco, CA: Jossey-Bass, 1997.

Hepburn, M. A. "Service-Learning and Civic Education in the Schools: What Does Recent Research Tell Us?" In *Education for Civic Engagement in Democracy: Service-Learning and Other Promising Practices*, edited by S. Mann and J. J. Patrick. Bloomington: Indiana University, ERIC Clearinghouse for Social Studies/Social Science Education, 2000.

Hodgkinson, V. A., and M. S. Weitzman. *Giving and Volunteering in the United States*. Washington, DC: Independent Sector, 1992.

Hodgkinson, V. A., and M. S. Weitzman. *Giving and Volunteering among American Teenagers 12 to 17 Years of Age*. Washington, DC: Independent Sector, 1992.

Kahne, J., and J. Westheimer. *The Limits of Efficacy: Educating Active Citizens for a Democratic Society*. New York, NY: Surdna Foundation, Inc, 2002.

Kyvig, D. E., and M. A. Marty. *Nearby History: Exploring the Past Around You*. Walnut Creek, CA: Rowman and Littlefield, 2000.

Lappe, R. M., and P. M. Dubois, P. M. *The Quickening of America: Rebuilding Our Nation, Remaking Our Lives*. San Francisco: Jossey-Bass, 1994.

Levison, L. *Community Service Programs in Independent Schools*. Boston, MA: National Association of Independent Schools, 1986.

Levstik, L. S., and K. C. Barton, K. C. *Doing History: Investigating with Children in Elementary and Middle Schools*, Third Edition. Mahwah, NJ: Erlbaum, 2005.

Maryland Student Service Alliance. *Maryland's Best Practices: An Improvement Guide for School-Based Service-Learning*. Baltimore, MD: Maryland Department of Education, 1995.

McAdam, D. "The Biographical Consequences of Activism." *American Sociological Review* 54 (1989): 744-759.

Melchior, A. *National Evaluation of Learn and Serve America School-Based Programs: Final Report*. Waltham, MA: Brandeis University Center for Human Resources and Abt Associates, 1998.

Melchior, A., J. Frees, L. LaCava, C. Kingsley, and J. Nahas. *Summary Report: National Evaluation of Learn and Serve America*. Waltham, MA: Center for Human Resources, Brandeis University, 1999.

Metz, E., J. McLellan, and J. Youniss. "Types of Voluntary Service and Adolescents' Civic Development." *Journal of Adolescent Research* 18, no. 2 (2003): 188-203.

Metz, E. C., and J. Youniss. "Longitudinal Gains in Civic Development through School-Based Required Service." *Political Psychology* 26, no. 3 (2005): 413-437.

Morgan, W., and M. Streb. "Building Citizenship: How Student Voice in Social-Learning Develops Civic Values." *Social Science Quarterly* 82, no. 1 (2001): 154-169.

National Council for the Social Studies. "Service-Learning: An Essential Component of Citizenship Education." *Social Education* 65, no. 4 (2001): 240-241.

Newmann, F. M. *Education for Citizen Action: Challenge for Secondary Curriculum*. Berkeley, CA: McCutchen, 1975.

Newmann, F. M., and R. A. Rutter. *The Effects of High School Community Service Programs on Students' Social Development*. Madison, WI: Wisconsin Center for Educational Research, University of Wisconsin, 1983.

Niemi, R., M. Hepburn, and C. Chapman. "Community Service by High School Students: A Cure for Civic Ills?" *Political Behavior* 22 (2000): 45-69.

Niemi, R. G., and J. Junn. *Civic Education: What Makes Students Learn*. Princeton, NJ: Yale University Press, 2005.

Noffke, S. "Action Research and Democratic Schooling: Problematics and Potentials." In *Educational Action Research: Becoming Practically Critical*, edited by S. E. Noffke & R. B. Stevenson, 1-10. New York: Teachers College Press, 1995.

Novak, J. M., ed. *Democratic Teacher Education: Programs, Processes, Problems, and Prospects*. Albany, NY: State University of New York Press, 1994.

Oliver, D. W. and J. P. Shaver. *Teaching Public Issues in the High School*. Boston: Houghton Mifflin, 1966.

Oja, S. N., and L. Smulyan. *Collaborative Action Research: A Developmental Approach*. London: Falmer, 1989.

Parker, W. C., ed., *Educating the Democratic Mind*. Albany, NY: State University of New York Press, 1996.

Parker, W. C. "Participatory Citizenship: Civics in the Strong Sense." *Social Education* 53 (1989): 353-354.

Parker, W. C. *Teaching Democracy: Unity and Diversity in Public Life.* New York: Teachers College Press, 2002.

Parker, W. C., and J. Jarolimek. *Citizenship and the Critical Role of the Social Studies.* Washington, DC: National Council for the Social Studies, 1984.

Patrick, J. J. "Introduction to Education for Civic Engagement in Democracy." In *Education for Civic Engagement in Democracy: Service Learning and Other Promising Practices*, edited by S. Mann and J. J. Patrick. Bloomington: Indiana University, ERIC Clearinghouse for Social Studies/Social Science Education, 2000.

Percoco, J. A. *A Passion for the Past: Creative Teaching of U.S. History.* Portsmouth, NH: Heinemann, 1998.

Perry, J., and M. C. Katula. "Does Service Affect Citizenship?" *Administration and Society* 33 (2001): 330-333.

Pratte, R. *The Civic Imperative: Examining the Need for Civic Education.* New York: Teachers College Press, 1988.

Putnam, R. D. *Bowling Alone: The Collapse and Revival of American Community.* New York: Simon and Schuster, 2000.

Raskoff, S. A., & R. A. Sundeen. "Community Service Programs in High Schools." *Law and Contemporary Problems* 62, no. 4 (2000): 73-111.

Riedel, E. "The Impact of High School Community Service Programs on Students' Feelings of Civic Obligation." *American Politics Research* 30, no. 5 (2002): 499-527.

Rosenthal, S., C. Feiring, and M. Lewis. "Political Volunteering from Late Adolescence to Young Adulthood: Patterns and Predictors." *Journal of Social Issues* 54, no. 3 (1998): 477-493.

Rutter, R. A., and F. M. Newmann. "The Potential of Community Service to Enhance Civic Responsibility." *Social Education* 53 (1989): 371-374.

Scales, P. C., and D. A. Blyth. "Effects of Service-Learning on Youth: What We Know and What We Need to Know." *Generator* (1997): 6-9.

Scales, P.C., D. A. Blyth, T. H. Berkas, and J. C. Kielsmeier. "The Effects of Service-Learning on Middle School Students' Social Responsibility and Academic Success." *Journal of Early Adolescence* 20, no. 3 (2000): 332-358.

Scales, P.C., and E. Rochlkepartain. *Community Service and Service-Learning in U.S. Public Schools: Findings from a National Survey.* Minneapolis: Search Institute, 2004.

Schervish, P.G., V. A. Hodgkinson, M. Gates, and associates. *Care and Community in Modern Society: Passing on the Tradition of Service to Future Generations.* Washington, DC: Independent Sector, 1995.

Sehr, D. T. *Education for Public Democracy.* Albany, NY: State University of New York Press, 1997.

Selwyn, D., and J. Maher. *History in the Present Tense: Engaging Students through Inquiry and Action.* Portsmouth, NH: Heinemann, 2003.

Shaver, J. P., ed. *Building Rationales for Citizenship Education.* Washington, DC: National Council for the Social Studies, 1977.

Shermis, S., and J. Barth. "Teaching for Passive Citizenship: A Critique of Philosophical Assumptions." *Theory and Research in Social Education* 10 (1982): 17-37.

Shor, I. *When Students Have Power: Negotiating Authority in a Critical Pedagogy.* Chicago: The University of Chicago Press, 1996.

Shumer, R. "Service, Social Studies, and Citizenship: Connections for the New Century." *ERIC Digest* (1999).

Shumer, R., and B. Belbas. "What We Know about Service Learning." *Education and Urban Society* 28 (1996): 208-223.

Skinner, R., and C. Chapman. *Service-Learning and Community Service in K-12 Public Schools.* Washington, D.C.: National Center for Education Statistics, 1999.

Soder, R., ed. *Democracy, Education, and the Schools.* San Francisco: Jossey-Bass, 1996.

Stagg, A. *Service-Learning in K-12 Public Education.* College Park, MD: CIRCLE, School of Public Affairs, 2004.

Wade, R., ed. *Building Bridges: Connecting Classroom and Community Through Service-Learning in Social Studies.* Bulletin 97. Washington, DC: National Council for the Social Studies, 2000.

Wade, R., ed. *Community Service-Learning: A Guide to Including Service in the Public School Curriculum.* Albany: State University of New York Press, 1997.

Wade, R. *CiviConnections Educators' Guide.* Iowa City, IA: The University of Iowa, 2004.

Wade, R., and D. Saxe. "Community Service-Learning in the Social Studies: Historical Roots, Empirical Evidence, Critical Issues." *Theory and Research in Social Education* 24, no. 4 (1996): 331-359.

Walker, T. "Service as a Pathway to Political Participation: What Research Tells Us." *Applied Developmental Science* 6, no. 4 (2002): 183-188.

Westheimer, J. *Pledging Allegiance: The Politics of Patriotism in America's Schools.* New York: Teachers College Press, 2007.

Westheimer, J., and J. Kahne. "Service-Learning Required." *Education Week*, January 26, 2000, www.educationweek.org/ew/ew.

Wirthlin Group. *The Prudential Spirit of Youth Community Survey.* Newark, NJ: The Prudential, 1995.

Wood, G. *Schools that Work.* New York: Dutton, 1992.

Wyman, Jr., R. M. *America's History through Young Voices: Using Primary Sources in the K-12 Social Studies Classroom.* Boston: Pearson, 2005.

Yates, M., and J. Youniss. "Community Service and Political Identity Development in Adolescents." *Journal of Social Studies* 54 (1998): 495-512.

Yates, M., and J. Youniss. *The Roots of Civic Identity: International Perspectives on Community Service and Activism in Youth.* Cambridge, UK: Cambridge University Press, 1999.

Yell, M., G. Scheurman, and K. Reynolds. *A Link to the Past: Engaging Students in the Study of History.* Bulletin 102. Silver Spring, MD: National Council for the Social Studies, 2004.

Youniss, J., J. A. McLellan, and M. Yates. "What We Know about Engendering Civic Identity." *American Behavioral Scientist* 40 (1997): 620-632.

Zarnowski, M. *History Makers: A Questioning Approach to Reading and Writing Biographies.* Portsmouth, NH: Heinemann, 2003.

Zemelman, S., P. Bearden, Y. Simmons, and P. Leki. *History Comes Home: Family Stories across the Curriculum.* York, ME: Stenhouse, 2000.

Zinn, H. *A People's History of the United States.* New York: Harper and Row, 1980.

Zinn, H., and A. Arnove, A. *Voices of a People's History of the United States.* New York: Seven Stories Press, 2004.

Civic Education Websites

CENTER FOR CIVIC EDUCATION (CCE)
www.civiced.org
This website offers information on CCE and its many civic education programs (such as "We the People..."), publications, articles and papers on civic education, research and evaluation, curricular materials, civics frameworks and standards, and sample lesson plans from CCE books.

CIVIC PRACTICES NETWORK (CPN)
www.cpn.org
CPN describes itself as "a collaborative and nonpartisan project bringing together a diverse array of organizations and perspectives within the new citizenship movement." The CPN website features case studies, essays, manuals, syllabi, and information about techniques and training in civic participation for public problem solving.

CIVNET
civnet.org
The mainstay of this site, published by CIVITAS (an international, non-governmental organization dedicated to promoting civic education), is a monthly journal of articles about the current state of democracy and civic education, reviews, and reports, all written by civic educators. A civic education resource library features on- and off-site links to historical documents, lesson plans, syllabi, bibliographies, research, journals, newsletters, and other materials. Also featured is a directory of civic education organizations around the world, a calendar of civic education events, and news about CIVITAS activities.

CLOSE UP FOUNDATION
www.closeup.org
The Close Up Foundation aims to teach "responsible participation in the democratic process through civic education programs and publications on government and citizenship." Their website offers information about Close Up's educational books, videos, games, and simulations; its travel programs and service learning programs for K-12 students and older Americans; the K-12 "Close Up Connections" program; and "Close Up on C-SPAN," a weekly public affairs/news program broadcast on C-SPAN.

CONSTITUTION SOCIETY
www.constitution.org
Explores rights, powers, and duties; abuses and usurpations; jurisdiction and due process; and the electoral process. Also provides information and additional links on citizen action, organizations, events, commentary, resources, United States founding documents, the concept of unity and federalism, constitutional defense, legal and political reform, public education, publications, people, references, and images.

CONSTITUTIONAL RIGHTS FOUNDATION (CRF)
www.crf-usa.org
The website of this community-based organization dedicated to educating young people for civic participation features an index and catalog to its publications, which include a K-12 curriculum on civic participation, service learning, government, law-related education, and mock trials and simulations. Also includes information about CRF teacher workshops and other programs.

C-SPAN ONLINE
www.c-span.org
Not just up-to-the-minute news on activities in Congress, but information on and materials for using C-SPAN in the classroom.

DEMOCRACYNET
www.ned.org
The website of the National Endowment for Democracy (NED) offers the Democracy Grants Database, the catalog of NED's Democracy Resource Center, information about Journal of Democracy and other NED publications, and instructions for subscribing to the electronic newsletter, DemocracyNews.

About the Authors

Sandy Arendt is a fifth grade teacher in the Princeton School District, Princeton, Wisconsin. Arendt has completed many service-learning projects with students that focus on the elderly and the environment.

Megan Baker is an eighth and ninth grade humanities teacher at Lincoln Junior High International Baccalaureate World School in Fort Collins, Colorado. Baker has authored several publications and has been active in curriculum development in the areas of environmental and geographic education.

Paul Doro is a fourth grade teacher in the Princeton School District, Princeton, Wisconsin. Doro has collaborated with the Lion's Club, the Princeton Library, and other community groups on service-learning activities.

Diane Gardner is a fourth grade teacher at Shenandoah Elementary School in Orlando, Florida. Gardner specializes in language arts and social studies and publishes student writing in a quarterly class newspaper.

Christine Harmon is a seventh grade social studies and language arts teacher at Newberry Middle School in Newberry, Michigan. Harmon was awarded the W.K. Kellogg Foundation Influential Educator Award in 1996 and 1997.

Litia Ho is an eighth grade teacher at Wai`anae Intermediate School in Hawaii. Ho's CiviConnections project was included in the poster sessions at the National Service-Learning Conference in 2005.

Jeanna Kooser is a seventh grade social studies teacher and social studies department head at Kalles Junior High in Puyallup, Washington. Kooser is responsible for the development and implementation of the 7th and 8th grade social studies curriculum and has participated in implementing Project Citizen in her school.

Linda Levstik is a professor in the Department of Curriculum and Instruction at the University of Kentucky in Lexington. Levstik has published extensively in the field of social studies education, and is co-author with Keith Barton of *Doing History* and *Teaching History for the Common Good* and co-editor with Cynthia Tyson of the upcoming *Handbook on Research in Social Education* (all published by Erlbaum).

Mark Lidtke is a seventh grade teacher at French Prairie Middle School in Woodburn, Oregon. In addition to teaching language arts and social studies, Lidtke has been active in staff development and curriculum reform in the Woodburn school district.

Thomas J. Scott teaches American government and citizenship, as well as world history, at Rosemount High School in Rosemount, Minnesota. Scott is the author of a variety of articles on citizenship education, information literacy and global education, and is an adjunct professor at Saint Mary's University in Minneapolis and Metropolitan State University in St. Paul.

Monica Sigala is a seventh grade social studies and language arts teacher at John Sutter Middle School in Fowler, California. A former AmeriCorps member, Sigala has been active in her school as a Community Service Club and yearbook advisor.

Lynn Smith teaches grades five through eight at Taylor County Middle School in Grafton, West Virginia. Smith has been awarded numerous grants to implement programs in her school and was selected as the 1997 Taylor County Teacher of the Year.

Kathy Steele teaches Gifted Social Studies courses for grades six through nine at Perry Local Schools in Massillon, Ohio. Steele also coordinates a high school mentorship program and is the advisor for the Senior Ohio Model United Nations teams.

Rahima C. Wade is Professor of Elementary Social Studies at The University of Iowa. Wade is author of more than fifty publications on service-learning, civic education, and social justice education. She served as Project Director of the CiviConnections program and was honored in 2004 by being selected as the John Glenn Scholar for Service-Learning in Teacher Education.

Index